LIKE A HOLY CRUSADE

*I have often been asked what it felt like to partici-
pate in such a movement. I can remember many
emotions—fear, anger, and sadness, but also hope,
love, and compassion. Most of all, there was an
all-pervading sense that one was involved in a
movement larger than oneself, almost like a Holy
Crusade, an idea whose time had come.*

> —John Lewis
> Chairman, Student Nonviolent
> Coordinating Committee, 1963–1966

Like a Holy Crusade

MISSISSIPPI 1964—THE TURNING OF

THE CIVIL RIGHTS MOVEMENT IN AMERICA

Nicolaus Mills

IVAN R. DEE
Chicago, 1992

LIKE A HOLY CRUSADE. Copyright © 1992 by Nicolaus Mills. All rights reserved, including the right to reproduce this book or portions thereof in any form. For information, address: Ivan R. Dee, Inc., 1332 North Halsted Street, Chicago 60622. Manufactured in the United States of America and printed on acid-free paper.

Library of Congress Cataloging-in-Publication Data:
Mills, Nicolaus.
    Like a holy crusade : Mississippi 1964—the turning of the civil rights movement in America / Nicolaus Mills.
        p.   cm.
    Includes bibliographical references and index.
    ISBN 0-929587-96-0
    1. Afro-Americans—Civil rights—Mississippi. 2. Civil rights movements—Mississippi—History—20th century. 3. Mississippi—Race relations. 4. United States—Race relations. I. Title.
E185.93.M6M55   1992
305.896′0730762—dc20   92-13846

For Irving Howe

Acknowledgments

We hear all the time that writing has become more and more like a competitive sport with writers treating one another as opponents. I have found the reverse to be true in my work on the Mississippi Summer Project. I received help from everyone I asked. Clayborne Carson, whose history *In Struggle: SNCC and the Black Awakening of the 1960s* has been invaluable reading for me, shared documents I did not have. Doug McAdam, whose book on the volunteers, *Freedom Summer*, has been no less crucial to my work, was equally generous in sharing materials and putting me in contact with volunteers I did not know. David Garrow did the kind of line-by-line criticism that is the equivalent of giving blood. For the time to complete my writing I owe much to a Hewlett-Mellon Grant from Sarah Lawrence College. Finally, I am greatly indebted to the following friends for help in my research and travels: Susannah Abbey, Therese Allen, Patsy Brumfield, Catherine Buchanan, Janet Cawley, Jack Chatfield, Allison Daugherty, Marlin Dooley, Samantha Fenrow, Erwin Flaxman, Marshall Ganz, Elinor Horner, Marilyn Lowen, Nicole Piscopo, Nancy Schieffelin, John Seidman, Meredith Silverstein, and Bob Struckman.

N. M.

New York City
May 1992

Contents

LIKE A HOLY CRUSADE

1

Introduction: Like a Holy Crusade

"Are you that nigger lover?"

It was not the first time Michael Schwerner had been called a nigger lover. Since coming to Mississippi in January 1964 he had constantly been taunted by angry whites in the small town of Meridian, where he and his wife worked at the local community center for the Congress of Racial Equality (CORE).

On this June night the question was not, however, just another taunt. It was after eleven. Schwerner was carrying two other civil rights workers in his station wagon—James Chaney, a twenty-one-year-old black CORE worker from Mississippi, and Andrew Goodman, a twenty-year-old Queens College student. They had just been stopped by two carloads of men led by Neshoba County Deputy Sheriff Cecil Price.

Earlier in the day the three civil rights workers had driven from Meridian to Longdale to inspect the ruins of the Mount Zion Methodist Church, which had been burned to the ground five days before after its congregation agreed it could be used as a Freedom School for teaching young black children. On their way back from the church, Schwerner, Chaney, and Goodman had been arrested by Price for speeding and kept in jail until ten o'clock. Now they were being stopped a second time. It was impossible for Schwerner not to know the danger they were in. In jail they had not been allowed to make a phone call. There was no way anyone in the Meridian CORE office could know where they were.

"Sir, I know just how you feel," Schwerner said to the man facing him. Perhaps Schwerner believed his answer would strike a soft spot? Perhaps he believed he could buy time?

A moment later a shot rang out, and Schwerner was dead. Another shot, and Andrew Goodman was dead. Then it was James Chaney's turn. The FBI's files do not tell us if Chaney also tried to speak. They do tell us that one of his killers shouted, "Save one for me!"[1]

A lynching was nothing new for Mississippi. But in the case of Schwerner, Chaney, and Goodman, the lynchers had made a mistake. They had not simply killed a black Mississippian willing to challenge their authority; they had also killed two whites from outside Mississippi. These were murders that could not be covered up. They were national news, and they would force the president and the FBI to act.

• • •

That a remote Mississippi crossroads had become America's crossroads was no accident. In the summer of 1964 Michael Schwerner, James Chaney, and Andrew Goodman were not just three young men doing civil rights work in Mississippi. They were part of a massive undertaking, the Mississippi Summer Project, designed to make sure that the civil rights movement in Mississippi became more than a war between the Mississippi power structure and an outnumbered coalition of blacks.

The idea behind the Mississippi Summer Project was as simple as it was daring. A task force of a thousand volunteers —most of them white, Northern college students—would be recruited to come to Mississippi for the summer. There they would work on voter registration, start Freedom Schools, and help build a political party, the Mississippi Freedom Democrats, open to all races. Without money, without power, without significant numbers the Summer Project would show, its organizers believed, that the segregationist laws keeping more than 90 percent of Mississippi's blacks from voting could be overcome. "We shall be as a city upon a hill," the Puritans had insisted before landing in America. For the Summer Project organizers, example too would be everything.[2]

In the summer of 1964 white Mississippi was, however, in no mood to accept a Second Reconstruction, especially one led by the coalition behind the Summer Project, the Council of Federated Organizations (COFO)—an alliance made up of the Congress of Racial Equality, the National Association for the Advancement of Colored People (NAACP), the Southern Christian Leadership Conference (SCLC), and, most important, the Student Nonviolent Coordinating Committee (SNCC), which provided three-fourths of the Summer Project staff. The *Jackson Clarion-Ledger* spoke for most of white Mississippi when it described the Summer Project as an invasion.[3]

In choosing Mississippi as the site for such an attack on segregation, the Summer Project organizers were aware of the level of opposition they would arouse. Between 1882 and 1952 Mississippi had been home to 534 reported lynchings, more than any other state in the nation; and with the start of the civil rights movement in the 1960s, lynchings in Mississippi took on added significance. The new target was no longer, as in the 1950s, a teenager like Emmett Till, who dared flirt with a white woman. The new target was a farmer like Herbert Lee, who showed that he was not afraid to be seen working with SNCC. For any white politician who wanted to get ahead, playing the race card was as important as it had been in the post-Reconstruction era. By Mississippi standards Governor Paul Johnson, Jr., was a moderate, but in 1964—a year in which 86 percent of all nonwhite families in Mississippi were living below the federal poverty line—no Johnson stump speech went over better than the one in which he declared that the initials of the NAACP stood for "niggers, apes, alligators, coons, and possums."[4]

"If we can crack Mississippi, we will likely be able to crack the system in the rest of the country," John Lewis, SNCC's chairman in 1964 and today a Georgia congressman, predicted as the Summer Project got under way. Lewis's thinking reflected the state of American race relations in 1964. Although the Interstate Commerce Commission had ruled in 1961 that segregation was illegal in all interstate public facilities, in practice an American apartheid prevailed throughout the Deep South. Especially in rural areas, blacks were likely to encounter segregation in everything from schools to water fountains. "If an American, because his skin is dark, cannot eat in a restaurant, cannot send his children to the best public school available, cannot vote for the elected officials who represent him, then who among us would be content to have the color of his skin changed and stand in his place?" President John Kennedy asked in 1963. A year later the answers to Kennedy's rhetorical question were still bitter ones. In 1964 the five normally Democratic states of the Deep South—Mississippi, Alabama, Louisiana, South Carolina, and Georgia—voted for conservative Barry Goldwater, believing that the Republicans now offered the best chance for them to maintain a situation in which only two million of the South's five million voting-age blacks were registered. The switch to Goldwater was a bold move, but it was buttressed by the assurance that as long as federal law remained what it was, the Justice Department could never sue enough registrars to weaken the South's ability to prevent most blacks from voting.[5]

In targeting Mississippi and making the most openly segregationist state in the Deep South a test case, the Summer Project organizers were not, however, attempting to turn themselves and the volunteers they had recruited into civil rights martyrs. Central to the strategy of the Mississippi Summer Project was the belief that once the day-to-day realities of Mississippi life were exposed, both the nation and the federal government would be forced to become deeply involved in the civil rights struggle.

It was not a naive assumption on the part of the Summer Project organizers. America in 1964 was prosperous and willing to look at itself in new ways. 1964 was a year of rising steel production and the new Ford Mustang, of the Beatles' American debut and Rudi Gernreich's topless bikini, of Stanley Kubrick's *Dr. Strangelove* and Philip Johnson's new wing at the Museum of Modern Art. But most of all 1964 was a year in which racial change was on everyone's mind. Cassius Clay (not yet Muhammad Ali) won the heavyweight boxing title and announced he was a Black Muslim. Martin Luther King, Jr., won the Nobel Peace Prize and in his acceptance speech spoke to the world about Mississippi. And in the presidential election of 1964, racial liberalism was, as it has not been since, a political advantage, helping Lyndon

Johnson defeat conservative Barry Goldwater, one of just eight Republican senators to vote against the 1964 Civil Rights Act, by 15.9 million votes.[6]

It was, nonetheless, desperation rather than a sense of optimism about the racial climate in Mississippi that was the basis for the Mississippi Summer Project. SNCC had been an active presence in Mississippi since 1961, when Bob Moses, a Harvard-educated teacher from New York City, then in his middle twenties, went to the small town of McComb to organize a voter registration drive. But after three years of struggle, SNCC was, in Moses's judgment, at a point of no return. SNCC's field secretaries had shown they could overcome threats and beatings to win local support, but they had not succeeded in getting significant numbers of blacks onto the voter rolls. Now the inroads they had made were, Moses believed, in danger of being wiped out if they did not gain outside help. SNCC's funds were running low, its Mississippi staff was exhausted, and the Kennedy administration, despite the president's pro–civil rights rhetoric, was providing little practical help.[7]

As 1963 drew to a close, the question for SNCC was where to turn. The Justice Department was not about to send federal marshals into Mississippi to protect civil rights workers on a day-to-day basis, nor were the established civil rights organizations about to increase their financial commitment to a state they doubted could be won. The one bright spot in the picture was the willingness of young college-educated whites to come to Mississippi for civil rights work. In the fall of 1963 COFO held a "Freedom Vote" to show what blacks in Mississippi would do if allowed to go to the polls, and as a result of help provided by one hundred students recruited from Stanford and Yale, scored an important political victory. The students and the media attention they brought with them kept the violence down. More than eighty thousand blacks cast symbolic freedom ballots in polling booths set up in churches, community centers, and barber shops within the black community. In a state where only 28,500 out of more than 422,000 eligible blacks were registered to vote, the Freedom Vote dramatized the role played by fear in Mississippi politics.[8]

In the judgment of Bob Moses, who would head the Summer Project, the best option for the coming year was to turn to white students again, and at a SNCC meeting in Greenville, Mississippi, in November 1963, Moses proposed a 1964 Summer Project that would make extensive use of white volunteers. Moses was not just being pragmatic in proposing an interracial Summer Project. He was also convinced that it was essential for whites to be involved in the civil rights movement. As he told the Greenville meeting, "It changes the whole complexion of what you're doing, so it isn't any longer Negro fighting white. It's a question of rational people against irrational people."[9]

For the college students whom the Summer Project would draw on, Moses's timing was perfect. As members of the baby-boom generation they had grown up at a time when the United States was the strongest and wealthiest nation in the world. They were worried less about their own individual futures, which seemed assured, than about what was happening in America. The Summer Project gave them a chance to act on their concern. As one volunteer observed, "I'm going because the worst thing after burning churches and murdering children is keeping silent." For the volunteers, the struggle in Mississippi would be the moral equivalent of war. They would not be "good Germans" and ignore the violence around them. In their eyes white Mississippians, not they, were the ones out of touch with the country's values. As volunteer Len Edwards, the son of California Congressman Don Edwards, said of his decision to go South, "It was the most American statement I could make."[10]

There were, however, great risks in Moses's Summer

Project strategy. SNCC's gains in Mississippi had come about because it insisted on organizing at the grassroots. A large-scale Summer Project which made wide use of white volunteers threatened that grassroots organizing process. It also threatened the pride that SNCC's black organizers had come to take in themselves. By using white volunteers to draw the country's attention to Mississippi, the Summer Project was in essence playing on racism to overcome racism, betting that the electorate would concern itself with black Mississippians if it saw white college students coming to their aid.

The summer ended with fewer than seventeen hundred blacks added to Mississippi's voter rolls, and in August the Summer Project received a bitter setback at the Democratic National Convention in Atlantic City when its plans for unseating the all-white Mississippi delegation were soundly defeated. For those in SNCC who had opposed the Summer Project at the outset, as well as for many in Mississippi, the results were hard to swallow. By the fall of 1964 they were far angrier than they had been at any time since SNCC came to Mississippi.[11]

The Summer Project would prove, however, to be anything but a failure. Long after the 1960s were over, the Kennedy men would be remembered as "the best and the brightest." The Mercury astronauts, despite the early failures of the space program, would be celebrated for having "the right stuff." But if anyone in the 1960s earned the right to be heroized, it was the men and women who risked their lives to carry out the Summer Project. That summer took a terrible toll on them. The project staff, the volunteers, above all the black families who opened their houses to the movement paid for their courage. In addition to the deaths of Schwerner, Chaney, and Goodman, there were thirty-seven church burnings, eighty beatings, and more than a thousand arrests of Summer Project workers by the end of August. Nonetheless, by the fall of 1964 white Mississippi, not the civil rights movement, was on the defensive in the eyes of most of the nation.[12]

Before the start of the Summer Project, Bob Moses made a point of telling his audiences that since January 1964 five blacks had been killed by whites in southwest Mississippi and nothing had been done about it. Once the Summer Project began, however, events in Mississippi no longer went unreported. When Schwerner, Chaney, and Goodman disappeared, it was front-page news. The president responded by sending the FBI to help search for them and calling for quick passage of the civil rights bill awaiting final congressional approval.[13]

In Mississippi the new Civil Rights Act and stepped-up federal involvement heightened the violence; but the violence, combined with the fact that in August the Summer Project was still operating, turned out to be an asset. It showed that Mississippi could be organized, its counterattacks weathered. The myth that Mississippi blacks were indifferent about voting or too passive to stand up for themselves was shattered. Sixty-five percent of the country had been opposed to the Summer Project before it began. But in the summer of 1964 the television cameras found news everywhere in Mississippi, and what the cameras showed left little credibility to the claims of Mississippi officials that their state was the victim of outside invaders whose aim was to provoke violence. The invaders looked too much like the middle-class college kids they were. The attacks on them and the black families sheltering them exposed, as no amount of public debate could have, what the Southern way of life meant in Mississippi.[14]

Several months later, when the Selma crisis began in March 1965, the country was ready for it in a way it had not been ready for the Summer Project. The sight of Alabama state troopers attacking civil rights marchers with clubs and tear gas as they marched in protest across the Pettus Bridge in Selma was Mississippi all over again, and the deaths of three Selma protesters, one black and two white, only added to the grim sense of déjà vu. In less than a month Selma was transformed from a local voter registration struggle into a national crisis, and the stage was set for the president to go before the country and propose the most far-reaching civil rights legislation of the 1960s, the Voting Rights Act of 1965.

A year later, as a result of the Voting Rights Act, there were more than 130,000 registered black voters in Mississippi, and by the early 1970s 268,440, or 62.2 percent of Mississippi's eligible black voters—tenfold the figure for 1964—were on the voter rolls. In less than a decade's time the most cherished political goal of the Summer Project was a reality.[15]

"I have often been asked what it felt like to participate in such a movement," John Lewis observed on the twentieth anniversary of the Summer Project. "Most of all, there was an all-pervading sense that one was involved in a movement larger than oneself, almost like a Holy Crusade, an idea whose time had come." Three decades after the Summer Project we seem about as far away from such feelings as it is possible to move. Today we are not surprised when the Leadership Conference on Civil Rights reports that the civil rights movement is seen by the electorate as pressing for the "narrow" concerns of "particularized" groups rather than opposing discrimination. We no longer ask, What happened to the civil rights movement? We know all too well what has happened to it since the mid-1960s—internal warfare, changes in leadership, the urban riots of the late 1960s, the busing crisis of the 1970s, the Rehnquist Court, the Reagan years. And, most recently, the Rodney King trial and Los Angeles riots of 1992.[16]

Our growing distance—political and emotional—from the Mississippi Summer Project of 1964 is, however, all the more reason to look closely at it. Since the Summer Project ended, we have seen two waves of writing about it. The first wave, which lasted from the mid-1960s to the mid-1970s, consisted largely of memoirs and firsthand accounts. The second wave, which occupied the 1980s, had a stronger historical focus, making use of such primary sources as FBI files, SNCC records, and volunteer applications to essay the impact of the Summer Project. Now, as we begin the 1990s, it is possible to widen the inquiry still further, to see what meaning the Summer Project has for us at a time when conservatives and liberals seem united in their gloom about race relations in America.[17]

These days it is all too tempting to remember the civil rights movement of the 1960s in ways that serve to excuse our current racial gridlock. We look back and see a movement that at its peak of public acceptance depended on larger-than-life leaders and was shaped by a white middle-class model of integration, and we throw up our hands in despair. What, we want to know, can such a movement teach us, except lessons we cannot use? How could it not have ended in racial schisms? The legacy of the Mississippi Summer Project challenges such memories in ways that offer hope. Here was a grassroots civil rights leadership that jokingly referred to Martin Luther King as "de Lawd" and shunned the kind of publicity that would have personalized its collective accomplishments. Here was a civil rights army in which—with most of the recruits white and most of the officers black—traditional notions about race and authority were constantly turned upside down.[18]

"Had the resources of eight hundred to a thousand students been held together," a Summer Project volunteer later said, "then I think with black and white together American history would have been different." We will never know. Perhaps such retrospective thinking is a fantasy of virtue? At a time when we have never had a more pressing need to find common racial ground, what we can know, however, is that the real tragedy of the Mississippi Summer Project is not that it failed but that so many of its participants gave up on it before its triumphs became clear.[19]

2

Burn Jim Crow
to the Ground

It is difficult to recall a political demonstration so associated with one man as the 1963 March on Washington. By the time he finished his "I have a dream" speech, the day was Martin Luther King's. The most prophetic speech given that hot August afternoon was not, however, King's. It was that of John Lewis, the new SNCC chairman. In his tone, in his deliberate distancing of himself from the civil rights establishment, Lewis forecast the event that in 1964 would transform the civil rights movement in the Deep South—the Mississippi Summer Project.

But it is with King, not Lewis, that the drama of the March on Washington begins. From the start King wanted his speech to be brief, "sort of a Gettysburg Address." He would, he knew, be following a long list of speakers. A fiery sermon would not do, not for this audience. The aim of the march was to pressure Congress into passing President Kennedy's civil rights bill. Demonstration, not civil disobedience, the march sponsors agreed, would be the order of the day. It was crucial to make sure the crowd that came to Washington stayed calm and did nothing to offend the congressmen on whom final passage of civil rights legislation depended. In an earlier meeting with the leaders of the march, the president had gone out of his way to warn against "the wrong kind of demonstration at the wrong time."[1]

Once King took the microphone and looked at the two hundred thousand people gathered around the reflecting pool of the Lincoln Memorial, however, he knew that neither he nor any of the march sponsors had imagined a gathering on this scale. Downtown Washington was deserted, but everywhere King looked there were people. They were even perched in the trees bordering the reflecting pool. The marchers had begun assembling at the Washington Monument in the early dawn. By 10:30 there were fifty thousand of them, by noon more than one hundred thousand. Opening the program, A. Philip Randolph, the seventy-four-year-old director of the march, announced, "We are gathered here in the largest demonstration in the history of this nation." King, too, was awed. As he waited for the applause that greeted him to die down, his movements were stiff, almost jerky. He started out reading his prepared speech; only after he had gotten through most of it did he begin to speak extemporaneously.[2]

It was a decision that made all the difference in the world. Until his "I have a dream" peroration, there was little in King's speech that moved his audience. He had tried too hard to write an updated Gettysburg Address. As he began reading from his prepared text, what emerged was not moral passion but historical self-consciousness. It was a speech so dominated by carefully crafted metaphors that it left little room for spontaneity. In Lincolnesque fashion King began, "Five score years ago, a great American, in whose symbolic shadow we stand today, signed the Emancipation Proclamation." Next came an even more elaborate historical reference—to the promissory note signed by the Founding Fathers when they wrote the Declaration of Independence and the Constitution. "It is obvious today that America has defaulted on this promissory note, insofar as citizens of color are concerned," King declared. "Instead of honoring this sacred obligation, America has given the Negro people a bad check, a check which has come back marked 'insufficient funds.' "[3]

"But we refuse to believe that the bank of justice is bankrupt," King continued. "*Now* is the time to make real the promises of Democracy. *Now* is the time to rise from the dark and desolate valley of segregation to the sunlit path of racial justice." Then, after a litany of all that was wrong with black life in America, King moved on to another appeal for action. "We cannot be satisfied so long as the Negro in Mississippi cannot vote and the Negro in New York believes he has nothing for which to vote," he insisted. "No, we are not satisfied, and we will not be satisfied until justice rolls down like waters and righteousness like a mighty stream."[4]

Once King began to speak of his dream, however, what he had to say became an altogether different story. "I'd used it many times before, that thing about 'I have a dream,' " King later acknowledged. But in the context of the March on Washington, there was nothing used about King's peroration. It transformed his words so that his speech no longer had a clear-cut beginning, middle, and end. It became instead a dialogue between him and the crowd. King offered a dream. The crowd answered back with applause. King responded with a new dream. It was no longer just civil rights that King was talking about now, it was civil religion—the nation's destiny as the accomplishment of God's will. God's purposes, American history, and the fate of the nation's black population became inseparable as King described his dream. His "I have a dream" refrain was the Bible made political, the Southern revivalist tradition linked to the idea of equality.[5]

King cited the Declaration of Independence, then pictured the sons of former slaves and the sons of former slave owners sitting down together at the table of brotherhood. He quoted Isaiah, "Every valley shall be exalted and every hill and mountain shall be made low," and imagined freedom ringing from "every hill and molehill of Mississippi." He called for the day when "all of God's children will be able to sing with new meaning, 'My country 'tis of thee, sweet land of liberty.' " And he ended by envisioning a future in which the entire nation would "join hands and sing in the words of the old Negro spiritual, 'Free at last. Free at last. Thank God, Almighty, we are free at last.' "[6]

King's vision took the country from its beginnings to the present, and as he repeated his "I have a dream" peroration (four times in the first paragraph that he used it, eight times in all), the momentousness of what he was saying began to build. Each dream stood on its own yet melted into the others. And as the process repeated itself, the hope King was expressing became more tenable. During the Revolution and later during the Civil War, the country had been tested, King made clear, as to whether it believed all men are created equal. Now it was being tested again, and it was not too much to think it could triumph again, that the heritage of Washington and Lincoln was alive in 1963.[7]

In the next day's *New York Times*, columnist James Reston summed up King's speech by comparing his words with those of Roger Williams, Sam Adams, Henry Thoreau, William Lloyd Garrison, and Eugene Debs. "Each time the dream was a promise out of our ancient articles of faith: phrases from the Constitution, lines from the great anthem of the nation, guarantees from the Bill of Rights, all ending with the vision that they might one day all come true," Reston wrote. It was the kind of front-page analysis political speeches rarely receive in this country, but King had created a context in which Reston's praise did not seem extravagant. By the time King finished, there was no base he had failed to touch. Built on repetition, his speech grew stronger as it was replayed on television in homes across the country. One did not have to be in the crowd at the Lincoln Memorial to identify with the hope it expressed.[8]

King's success at the March on Washington was especially crucial for the civil rights movement. Plans for the march had been in the works since 1962, when A. Philip Randolph, the founder and president of the Brotherhood of Sleeping Car Porters, proposed a "mass descent" on Washington that would draw public attention to the economic plight of blacks in America and the need for more civil rights legislation. But by early 1963 it seemed unlikely that such a march would happen. Randolph could not get other civil rights leaders to agree that the time was right. Only in June, when Martin Luther King concluded that the civil rights demonstrations he had been leading in Birmingham against Public Safety Commissioner Bull Connor and the city's merchants needed the support of national protests, did prospects for holding the march revive. Even then, the civil rights leadership was divided over how the march should be conducted and who should pay for it. The expense problem was removed when Stephen Currier, president of the liberal Taconic Foundation, proposed the establishment of the Council for United Civil Rights Leadership (CUCRL), which would serve as a clearing house for allocating the larger contributions that Currier himself promised to solicit on behalf of the march. But not until June 24 was the date for the march set, and even then infighting continued. The NAACP's Roy Wilkins objected to the appointment of Bayard Rustin as director of the march because Rustin had spent time in prison for refusing to serve in the army and had an arrest record for homosexuality. (Rustin was instead given the title of deputy director.) The leadership of SNCC was unhappy with the decision of the march sponsors to forbid civil disobedience.[9]

King's speech did not erase such internal differences, but it did deflect public attention from what divided the march's black leaders, who, in addition to Randolph and King, included Roy Wilkins of the NAACP, John Lewis of SNCC, James Farmer of CORE, and Whitney M. Young, Jr., of the National Urban League. King's vision of a civil rights movement rooted in a belief in American justice forced the public and the media to think about the reasons for the march. After King finished speaking, it was easy for Bayard Rustin to step to the podium and get the crowd to roar its approval of the goals of the march. The nation was put in the same position. In the face of King's dream, it seemed petty to dwell on the divisions among the march's six black sponsors.[10]

King's speech also furthered the kind of biracial coalition which the established civil rights movement believed was needed in order to get action from Congress. In addition to the black sponsors of the march, there were four key whites: Walter Reuther, president of the United Automobile Workers; Matthew Ahmann, director of the National Catholic Conference for Interracial Justice; Rabbi Joachim Prinz, president of the American Jewish Congress; and the Reverend Eugene Carson Blake from the National Council of Churches. King's speech not only said they were welcome; it said that in a country where racial justice was both a religious and a secular concern, the kinds of organizations these men represented had an obligation to participate in the civil rights movement.[11]

Finally, King's triumph at the March on Washington was crucial for the Kennedy administration. The relationship between King and Kennedy had become extremely complicated by 1963. During the 1960 presidential campaign Kennedy publicly intervened to have King released from a Georgia jail. In 1963, when King was jailed in Alabama, Kennedy acted again, this time calling his wife Coretta King to assure her that the FBI had ascertained that her husband was safe. The calls earned Kennedy the gratitude of the King family as well as a great many black votes. But the calls did not make King look the other way when the Kennedy administration sought to keep "order" in the South rather than support black protest. In early June, King made headlines when he described the president's record on civil rights as "inadequate" and charged him with not living up to his campaign promises.[12]

Only reluctantly did the president commit himself to supporting the March on Washington. It was not until June 22, after plans for an August march were announced, that the president asked its leaders to the White House. At that meeting he did everything in his power, short of asking them to call off the march, to discourage them from going ahead with it. "It seemed to me a great mistake to announce a March on Washington before the [civil rights] bill was even in committee," the president told the march leaders. "Now we are in a new phase, the legislative phase, and results are essential. . . . We have, first, to oppose demonstrations which will lead to violence, and, second, give Congress a fair chance to work its will." Three weeks passed before the president gave his formal blessing to the march. In doing so, he pointed out to the press that he viewed it as "not a march on the capital" but a "peaceful assembly calling for a redress of grievances."[13]

Kennedy was gambling. By blessing the march in advance, he wanted to make sure that its target would be the Southern senators who opposed his civil rights bill and not his own record on civil rights. The national reaction to King's "I have a dream" speech redeemed that strategy. The optimism of King's speech, its equation of civil rights and Americanism, was tailor-made to the political image the Kennedy administration wished to project. The order maintained by the marchers added to that image. Neither the two thousand National Guardsmen called to duty in Washington nor the troops standing by in Maryland and Virginia needed to be brought to the march. Indeed, there was scarcely a need for the twenty-nine hundred Washington police whose leaves were canceled on the day of the march. A five-hundred-man cleanup squad organized by Bayard Rustin picked up the trash the huge crowd had left behind. At the end of the day the president no longer had to worry that he had made a mistake in supporting the march. He could share in the march's triumph by inviting its leaders to the White House and announcing, "This nation can properly be proud of the demonstration that has occurred here today. The leaders of the organizations sponsoring the march and all who have participated in it deserve our appreciation for the detailed preparations that made it possible and for the orderly manner in which it has been conducted."[14]

As he listened to the speeches that day and watched the marchers (three-fourths of whom, a Bureau of Social Science Research survey would reveal, held white-collar jobs), Malcolm X, then at the height of his influence as a black nationalist, was horrified. The meticulous organization that so impressed reporters—eighty thousand prepared lunches, fifteen hundred volunteer marshals, printed picket signs— struck Malcolm as proof of how thoroughly the march leaders had caved in to white demands. "Who ever heard of angry revolutionaries swinging their bare feet together with their oppressor in lily pad pools, with gospels and guitars and 'I have a dream' speeches?" Malcolm later wrote in his *Autobiography.* "There wasn't a single logistics aspect uncontrolled. The marchers had been instructed to bring no signs—signs were provided. They had been told to sing one song: 'We Shall Overcome.' They had been told *how* to arrive, *when, where,* to arrive, where to assemble, when to *start* marching, the *route* to march."[15]

Malcolm X was not the only black leader with doubts about the march. For very different reasons John Lewis of SNCC was also skeptical. At twenty-five the youngest of the march sponsors, Lewis was initially ignored by most of the press and the other march leaders. The Sunday before the march, the *New York Times Magazine* printed a symposium on what black leaders wanted, but neither Lewis nor SNCC was asked to participate, and when the time came to divide the money that had been raised for the civil rights organizations sponsoring the march, SNCC also found itself shortchanged. While the NAACP and the Urban League received $125,000 each and King's Southern Christian Leadership Conference $50,000, SNCC, whose field secretaries in Mississippi were risking their lives daily, was given only $15,000.[16]

What was most troubling to Lewis about the march was not, however, its logistics or how SNCC was treated financially. Rather, it was the compromises that the march sponsors were prepared to make in order to maintain unity and gain the support of the Kennedy administration. As he began his own speech that day, Lewis did not share Martin Luther King's feeling that here was the audience of a lifetime. The constituency that John Lewis spoke for was, as far as he was concerned, already on the front lines in the South. It simply wasn't receiving the attention that King's protests in Montgomery and Birmingham had generated. By contrast, SNCC's voter registration efforts in Mississippi had quickly passed from the front pages, despite the fact that in rural McComb they had led to more than 120 arrests and in Greenwood they had resulted in the shooting—and near murder—of a SNCC field secretary. Even the murder of Amite County farmer and SNCC supporter Herbert Lee had not provoked much public attention outside Mississippi.[17]

In addressing the March on Washington, Lewis saw his task as one of shattering illusions and setting the record straight. What preoccupied him was all that he saw missing from the march. "We march today for jobs and freedom, but we have nothing to be proud of," were Lewis's first words. "For hundreds and thousands of our brothers are not here. . . . They have no money for their transportation, for they are receiving starving wages or no wages at all. While we stand here, there are sharecroppers in the Delta of Mississippi who are out in the fields working for less than three dollars a day for twelve hours of work."[18]

Few at the march and still fewer watching it on television were prepared for Lewis's anger. But as he warmed to his task, Lewis made no attempt to close the distance he had staked out in his opening paragraph. In contrast to King, who would wait for applause before moving on to a new idea, Lewis proceeded at his own pace, barely pausing to catch his breath between paragraphs. The Kennedy administration and the moderate tone of the march were his next targets. "It is true that we support the present civil rights bill in Congress. We support it with great reservations, however. Unless Title Three is put in this bill, there is nothing to protect young children and old women from police dogs and fire hoses, their penalty for engaging in peaceful demonstrations," Lewis declared. "As it stands now the voting section of this bill will not help thousands of black people who want to vote." Blacks in America were at the end of their patience, Lewis warned. It was now up to the federal government to intervene on their behalf or face the consequences. "To those who have said be patient and wait, we must say that we cannot be patient, we do not want to be free gradually. We want our freedom and we want it now," Lewis insisted. Then, in a Founding Fathers reference very different from King's gentle allusion, Lewis went on to conclude, "All of us must get in this great social revolution sweeping our nation. Get in and stay in the streets of every city, every village, and every hamlet of this nation until true freedom comes, until the unfinished revolution of 1776 is complete."[19]

Lewis's most powerful criticisms were not, however, spoken at the Lincoln Memorial; they were written into the speech he prepared for delivery, then changed. An advance copy of Lewis's speech had been read by Attorney General Robert Kennedy and his assistant for civil rights, Burke Marshall, then passed on to Patrick Cardinal O'Boyle, the Catholic prelate scheduled to give the invocation at the march. O'Boyle's objection to the speech was similar to Kennedy's, and he threatened to withdraw from the march unless Lewis changed his militant language. When news of Cardinal O'Boyle's reaction reached Bayard Rustin on Tuesday, Rustin called a meeting of the march sponsors and that night met with Lewis in an effort to persuade him to change his text. Lewis refused, believing then, as he would continue to believe years later, "If the cardinal had not objected, nobody would have paid attention." By early Wednesday morning, with the march just hours away, the dispute continued.

O'Boyle's objections put Rustin in a difficult position. The cardinal wanted specific deletions that reflected not only Lewis's thinking but that of Tom Kahn, Rustin's aide, who had helped draft the speech. But to lose O'Boyle's support at this juncture would be to lose the kind of unity the march was designed to achieve. O'Boyle warned that if the changes in Lewis's speech were not made he and the other religious leaders would leave the march. Finally, with the start of the march only minutes away, Lewis agreed to change his speech "in the name of unity." In a small room just behind the statue of Lincoln, Lewis and SNCC staffers James Forman and Courtland Cox worked out a new speech that would meet the cardinal's demands.[20]

Lewis's decision to change his speech did not, however, persuade him that his original draft had been a mistake. The militancy of that draft ran deep. Lewis was among the SNCC leaders who wanted demonstrations at the Justice Department to be included in the march plans, and he believed then, as he would observe more than two decades later, "The speech was very much in keeping with American ideals." Certainly nothing in the original draft would have come as a surprise to anyone who knew the commitment Lewis had made to the civil rights movement, beginning with the Nashville sit-ins of 1960. But there was an unmistakable difference in the quality of Lewis's two speeches. In the speech he delivered, Lewis was not at his best. He was struggling not only to keep a lid on his emotions but to express himself in language that fell short of what he wanted to say.[21]

The draft speech was a different story. There Lewis spoke for a SNCC that was skeptical of the Kennedys and believed, as James Forman later wrote, that the administration wanted the march "to take the steam out of the black anger then rising in the South." At the march Lewis softened his doubts about the president's civil rights bill, first announcing that SNCC supported the bill, then announcing that it had reservations. In his draft, on the other hand, Lewis felt no need for such qualification: "In good conscience we cannot support, wholeheartedly, the administration's civil rights bill, for it is too little, and too late," he declared. "There is not one thing in the bill that will protect our people from police brutality."[22]

By the end of the 1960s it would be customary for any black leader who wished to be seen as militant to attack liberal civil rights legislation, but there was nothing contrived about the anger in Lewis's undelivered speech. His was not the kind of put-on protest that Tom Wolfe would later characterize as "mau-mauing" the white man. In style and substance the passages that so upset Cardinal O'Boyle matched Lewis's politics. It was General Sherman in Georgia, not Abraham Lincoln at Gettysburg, "The Battle Hymn of the Republic" rather than soothing black spirituals, that Lewis wanted his Washington audience to think about. As his original text made clear in the bluntest possible language, Lewis believed that the real problem for blacks in the South was not Southern politicians so much as the American political system itself. "This nation is still a place of cheap political leaders who build their careers on immoral compromises and ally themselves with open forms of political, economic, and social exploitation. What political leader here can stand up and say, 'My party is the party of principles'?" Lewis asked. The party of John Kennedy, he pointed out, was also the party of Mississippi's James Eastland, and while the two men seemed like opposites, their conduct was often similar. The president, Lewis argued, had not merely proposed a civil rights bill that was inadequate, he was doing his best to slow the pace of black protest. "The [black] revolution is a serious one. Mr. Kennedy is trying to take the revolution out of the street and put it into the courts," Lewis charged. "I want to know, which side is the federal government on?"[23]

There was no turning back the forces unleashed by the civil rights movement, Lewis insisted, and in the conclusion of his draft speech, the section that most offended Cardinal

O'Boyle, Lewis predicted what blacks would and should do. "Listen Mr. Kennedy, listen Mr. Congressman, listen fellow citizens, the black masses are on the march for jobs and freedom, and we must say to the politicians that there won't be a 'cooling-off' period," Lewis warned. In his final paragraph Lewis assumed the voice of a modern Jeremiah, predicting that the civil rights revolution of the 1960s would conquer the South much as the Civil War had. By comparison with King's language, Lewis's language here was spare, a march tune rather than a hymn. But Lewis too could use metaphor, and there was no mistaking the threat in his deliberately repetitive syntax ("We will"/"We shall" each key sentence began). "The time will come when we will not confine our marching to Washington," Lewis proclaimed. "We will march through the South, through the heart of Dixie, the way Sherman did. We shall pursue our own 'scorched earth' policy and burn Jim Crow to the ground— nonviolently. We shall fragment the South into a thousand pieces and put them back together in the image of democracy. We will make the action of the past few months look petty."[24]

In a confidential memorandum written in early September 1963, Eleanor Holmes Norton, at the time a Yale law student working with SNCC (later the head of the Equal Employment Opportunity Commission), offered an upbeat assessment of SNCC's role in the march. "SNCC should not abandon its radicalizing role at this juncture," she concluded. It can "keep sell-outs from happening." John Lewis was even more optimistic about the impact that he and SNCC had had on the march. In his year-end report to SNCC, Lewis looked back on the march and observed of the controversy his speech had caused: "Since that time I find that people are asking questions about SNCC. What is SNCC's program? What is SNCC doing? Who is SNCC? And usually when they find out, they want in some way or another to become identified with SNCC. For this we can thank our good brethren, Archbishop O'Boyle, Messrs. Wilkins, King, Young, and Randolph. So much for that!"[25]

Like Eleanor Holmes Norton's view of the march, Lewis's was one shared by few outside SNCC. In less than a year it would be clear, however, that while the drama of the March on Washington belonged to Martin Luther King, its prophetic voice belonged to John Lewis. In signaling SNCC's break with the cautious liberalism of the early 1960s, Lewis had forecast both the strategy and the tone of the next stage of civil rights activity in the South. The compromises made by the March on Washington sponsors in order to win popular support would no longer be the way of the future. By June 1964 the civil rights movement had a new cutting edge. It was no longer led by the lawyers of the NAACP or the ministers of SCLC but by a generation of young SNCC field secretaries, most of them still in their twenties. And as at the March on Washington, the initial reaction of the media and the White House was to underestimate them, to assume that their plans for transforming the civil rights movement were too daring to succeed.

3

Tremor in the Iceberg

It was a letter that quickly became part of the Bob Moses legend. "We are smuggling this note from the drunk tank of the county jail in Magnolia, Mississippi. Twelve of us are here, sprawled out along the concrete bunker," Moses wrote. "It's mealtime now; we have rice and gravy in a flat pan, dry bread and a 'big town cake'; we lack eating and drinking utensils. Water comes from a faucet and goes into a hole. This is Mississippi, the middle of the iceberg. . . . This is a tremor in the middle of the iceberg—from a stone that the builders rejected."[1]

Three years later, in 1964, the letters coming out of Mississippi by civil rights workers doing time in jail would sound very similar. Low key, ironic, confident rather than fearful, the letters elevated defiance into a style. Anyone reading them could not fail to see the way they made a Mississippi jail sentence a rite of passage. For the 1964 civil rights workers, there would, however, be the added assurance that their letters were certain to be read, that the country, not just their families, cared about what was happening to them. "No action today from COFO, but the most active day yet for me inside the jail," a typical letter went. "The Deputy volunteered me the use of a razor after I asked and received permission to take a shower. Result: using a broken rearview mirror, my worst shave ever. . . . After the shower I had time to talk to the Negro prisoners in their cell. . . . They gave me a whole bunch of Superman comics. I also read the Book of Amos aloud. I don't know if anyone listened enough to get the point."[2]

The confidence reflected by the 1964 letters was no accident. It was a direct result of the work of Bob Moses, now director of the Mississippi Summer Project. Under Moses's leadership the lonely guerrilla war waged by SNCC in Mississippi since 1961 had been transformed into a struggle in which SNCC now had on its side a coalition of civil rights groups plus an army of a thousand volunteers—most of them Northern, most of them white, most of them college students.

Moses's commitment to a Summer Project was a gamble based on the belief that college students could be persuaded to spend a summer in Mississippi and that their presence there would galvanize the country into political action. "These students bring the rest of the country with them," Moses insisted. "They're from good schools, and their parents are influential. The interest of the country is awakened, and when that happens, the government responds to that interest."[3] The biggest gamble of the Summer Project would not, however, turn on the willingness of college students to risk their lives and come to Mississippi. It would turn on whether those who came to Mississippi as volunteers could do so without undermining SNCC and the local black leadership it had been nurturing.

Hollis Watkins, one of Bob Moses's cellmates in the Magnolia jail, was far from alone in his belief that a massive influx of volunteers with "no real understanding of what the South was like and no understanding of what had gone on" was a threat to the movement. From the time the Summer Project was conceived, it faced deep opposition within SNCC, especially from Mississippi-born organizers like Watkins who felt that "once the Summer Project was over, those of us who were left in Mississippi would be back at square one, having to re-create the wheel that at one point we had created."[4]

In their belief that Mississippi was, as SNCC Chairman John Lewis put it, "the stronghold of the whole vicious system of segregation," the organizers of the Summer Project and their opponents shared common ground. Since the end of the Civil War white Mississippi had prided itself on creating an environment in which blacks lived in constant fear. "We must keep the ex-slave in a position of inferiority. We must pass such laws as will make him feel his inferiority," the *Jackson Daily News* observed shortly after Mississippi elected its first postbellum legislature. For the next hundred years the state's leading newspapers and leading politicians echoed such sentiments. "Nigger voting, holding office, and sitting in the jury box are all wrong, and against the sentiment of the country," the *Columbus Democrat* argued on the eve of the election of 1875. An editorial in the *Jackson Clarion-Ledger* went even further, declaring, "If every Negro in Mississippi was a graduate of Harvard and had been elected class orator, he would not be as well fitted to exercise the rights of suffrage as the Anglo-Saxon farm laborer."[5]

The Mississippi Constitution of 1890, with its voting restrictions and poll tax, embodied such thinking, and as the new century began, so did Mississippi's harsh vagrancy and contract labor laws. As late as the 1930s, as Neil McMillen notes in his *Dark Journey: Black Mississippians in the Age of Jim Crow*, the NAACP was turning up in Mississippi cases of peonage—black laborers forced to work on plantations in order to repay debts they were said to owe. In this atmosphere race-baiting continued to be the key to political success for white politicians. Mississippi's turn-of-the-century governor, James K. Vardaman, did not hesitate to describe the black man as "a lazy, lying, lustful animal, which no conceivable amount of training can transform into a tolerable citizen." In his 1946 Senate reelection campaign, Eugene Bilbo, Vardaman's political heir, continued the same kind of race-baiting, telling white voters, "Do not let a single nigger vote. If you let a few register and vote this year, next year there will be twice as many, and the first thing you know, the whole thing will be out of hand."[6]

By the start of the 1960s little had changed in the way Mississippi politics were run. The new governor of Mississippi was Ross Barnett, who, like his predecessors, believed Mississippi must remain a white man's state. "If we start with the self-evident proposition that white and colored are different, we will not experience any difficulty in reaching the conclusion that they are not and never can be equal," Barnett declared. He did his best to enforce his declaration. In 1962 it took twenty thousand federal troops to enroll James Meredith, a black air force veteran, in the University of Mississippi, and in 1964, when Barnett left office, fewer Mississippi blacks were registered to vote than at the start of Reconstruction. Barnett's successor as governor, Paul Johnson, Jr., based his election campaign on defiance of the federal government and in his speeches routinely attacked the NAACP in vicious fashion.[7]

Recognizing the need for a black voter registration drive in Mississippi and actually starting one were, however, two very different matters. To begin with, violence had led to more black lynching deaths in Mississippi than in any other state. In earlier times the victims had been "uppity niggers." Now they were political leaders like Medgar Evers, Jackson's charismatic NAACP field secretary, who was murdered just hours after President Kennedy delivered the nationwide speech that set the stage for his proposal of what became the Civil Rights Act of 1964. As novelist and ex-Mississippian Walker Percy observed, "If their record in Lee's army is unsurpassed for valor and devotion to duty, present-day Mississippi is mainly known for murder, church-burning, dynamiting, assassination, night riding." Even Mississippi judges were willing to threaten civil rights workers. "Every effort you make to stir up violence in this community will be met," Bob Moses and two SNCC workers were told by the judge sentencing them to jail in 1961. "Some of you are local residents, some are outsiders. Those of you who are local residents are like sheep being led to the slaughter. If you continue to follow the advice of outside agitators, you will be like sheep and slaughtered."[8]

The threat of violence, coupled with the fact that Mississippi juries (blacks did not serve on them in the early 1960s) would not convict a white man accused of a racial murder, was the most chilling obstacle SNCC faced in trying to build a political movement in Mississippi. But most of the time, violence was a last resort. The usual tactic for stopping black protest before it started was economic pressure. In a state in which the median annual income of a black family was $1,444 in 1960, economic pressure was easy to apply. In rural areas where chopping cotton paid three dollars a day and most blacks sharecropped or lived in rented houses, trying to vote could mean financial ruin. When Fannie Lou Hamer, who later become one of the leaders of the Mississippi Freedom Democratic party, attempted to register in 1962, she was not only fired from her job as a plantation timekeeper, she and her family were forced to move from their house. Even the small number of black farmers who owned their own land and equipment and were not in debt were vulnerable to pressure to stay away from the polls. The White Citizens Councils, which had formed in Mississippi in 1954 in response to the Supreme Court's desegregation decision in *Brown* v. *Board of Education*, and consisted of the respectable members of the community—bankers, merchants, lawyers—were able to bring most independent farmers into line by seeing to it that their insurance was canceled or their credit denied. Scarcely any black family could avoid this sort of pressure. And as a last resort, there was always mass economic reprisal. When blacks in Greenwood attempted a voter education drive, the white supervisors of surrounding Leflore County retaliated by voting to withdraw their community from the federal programs on which most of the local black population depended for survival.[9]

As if all these difficulties were not enough, blacks in Mississippi had very few resources at their disposal in 1964. Especially in the countryside they were a population that had been beaten down for generations, with many still living as a landless peasantry. "We have to operate on the fact that all the people on the plantations in the Delta are expendable," Bob Moses acknowledged. "They're a surplus people as far as their labor is concerned, and not only that, they're unemployable people once they leave that plantation." Between 1950 and 1960 more than 315,000 blacks left Mississippi, and the population that remained was poorly fixed to take care of its needs. In her 1968 autobiography, *Coming of Age in Mississippi*, Anne Moody describes growing up in a house

in which "we never set a table because we never had but one
fork or spoon each." But for a family like Moody's, no less
daunting than their poverty was the task of finding a doctor
or a dentist or a lawyer. In 1959, according to NAACP
figures, there were in all of Mississippi only one black
dentist, five black lawyers, and sixty black doctors. And
there was no sign of this situation changing. If a black child
managed to survive birth—and the odds were 200 percent
greater than for Mississippi whites that he would not—he
faced a bleak future. As the 1960s began Mississippi not only
ran a segregated school system but spent three times more on
white than on black students. By the time they were finished
with their education (six years on average), most young
Mississippi blacks were qualified for only one kind of work—
the backbreaking manual labor that held 86 percent of their
parents below the poverty line.[10]

Given these circumstances it was reasonable for the organizers of the Mississippi Summer Project to believe, as Bob
Moses argued, "If we get a real breakthrough in voting
in Mississippi, we will spur Negro voting throughout the
South."[11] The hard part was figuring out what it would take
to achieve that breakthrough.

McComb provided SNCC with its first indication of how
tough civil rights work in Mississippi would be. At the
invitation of C. C. Bryant, head of the Pike County chapter
of the NAACP, Bob Moses arrived in McComb in July 1961.
On August 7 he began holding voter registration classes, and
by the end of his first week of classes, six of the sixteen
people he had taken to the county courthouse to register
made it onto the voter rolls. In a town where there were only
250 black voters out of a population of twelve thousand, six
new voters were enough to rate a story in the *McComb*

Enterprise-Journal. The following week black farmers in the adjoining counties of Amite and Walthall asked Moses to start voter registration classes there.[12]

It was an invitation Moses felt he should not refuse, but it also meant the start of much more serious trouble. On August 15, after unsuccessfully trying to register three people from Amite County, Moses was arrested and forced to spend two days in jail. Two weeks later, after another trip to the Amite courthouse, he was badly beaten by the cousin of the local sheriff. The next day Moses filed charges, but at the trial it was he who again became the victim. His assailant was acquitted, and after a mob formed outside the courthouse, Moses and his two witnesses were forced to flee the county under police escort.

Meanwhile, tensions were also rising in McComb. SNCC's operations there had increased with the arrival of new staff, many of whom had participated in the Nashville sit-in movement. The latter quickly began workshops in nonviolence, and on August 26 two of the workshop's participants were arrested for sitting-in at Woolworth's. Several days later three high school students were arrested for sitting-in at the still segregated Greyhound bus station.[13]

The arrests momentarily brought voter registration activity in McComb to a halt, but by late September tensions were again on the rise. On September 26 Herbert Lee, an Amite County farmer who had driven Bob Moses around the countryside while he was canvassing, was killed. His assailant, State Representative E. H. Hurst, claimed that Lee had come after him with a tire iron. It was a story shot through with holes (an eyewitness later reported that Lee had no tire iron), but to a local coroner's jury all that mattered was Hurst's version of events. On the same afternoon of the shooting, the jury ruled the killing a justifiable homicide.

Lee's death quickly became a source of anger in McComb. On October 4, when students who had been arrested

at the Greyhound bus station were refused entrance to Mc-
Comb's all-black Bergland High School, their suspension
plus Lee's death set off a protest rally. More than a hundred
students took to the streets in a demonstration that brought
them first to SNCC's office at the Masonic Lodge in Mc-
Comb and then to city hall. By the end of the day 119 of the
students, as well as Bob Moses and two SNCC workers,
Chuck McDew and Bob Zellner, were behind bars, and the
next day McComb authorities arrested all but one of the
remaining SNCC staffers. It was not until singer Harry
Belafonte sent five thousand dollars in bail money a few days
later that everyone was released.[14]

Leaving jail, Bob Moses went to Atlanta to attend a
SNCC meeting, then immediately returned to McComb with
sufficient staff to begin a "nonviolent high school" for the
Bergland High students who had been suspended from class.
It was a stopgap measure but enough to buoy the spirits of the
students until arrangements could be made for them to
complete their education at Campbell Junior College in
Jackson, which offered high school courses. Moses and the
SNCC staff could do little else in view of their own situation.
In November, as a result of their participation in the October
4 student demonstrations, they began serving sentences that
kept them in jail until early December.[15]

Moses would look back on McComb and observe, "We
had, to put it mildly, got our feet wet. We now knew
something of what it took to run a voter registration campaign in Mississippi; we knew some of the obstacles we
would have to face; we had some general idea of what had to
be done to get such a campaign started." But there were still
many reasons to be worried. McComb showed that local communities would not hesitate to make mass arrests and that
in short order precious bail money could be exhausted.
McComb also demonstrated that the federal government could
not be relied on in a crisis. John Doar of the Civil Rights

Division of the Justice Department had risked his life to come to McComb to investigate what was going on, but he had not been able to persuade Justice to take up the case of Herbert Lee or to offer SNCC any assurances of protection. After one death and four months of sacrifice, the movement in McComb came to a halt with fewer than two dozen new black voters on the rolls.[16]

In the wake of McComb, Bob Moses began 1962 convinced that the only way for SNCC to organize a voter registration campaign in Mississippi was to build it around a staff of "young people who would not be responsible economically to any sector of the white community and who would be able to act as free agents." It was a sound strategy, and in May 1963 when Moses testified at civil rights hearings held by the House Judiciary Committee, he could point to what SNCC had accomplished. In six Mississippi counties SNCC had twenty field secretaries, seventeen of whom were native Mississippians, working full time. But a sound strategy did not guarantee breakthroughs in voting. After McComb the Mississippi legislature added a requirement that the names of new voter applicants must be published in the newspapers for two weeks, and throughout the state resistance to the civil rights movement stiffened. In a December 1962 report to the Voter Education Project, which had helped supply SNCC with funding to carry out its work, Moses acknowledged, "We are powerless to register people in significant numbers anywhere in the state."[17]

The problems faced by SNCC in Mississippi in 1962 and 1963 were epitomized by its campaign in the Delta town of Greenwood. SNCC workers arrived there on August 15, 1962, and two days later were forced to flee their office in the middle of the night to avoid a mob. Their troubles were, however, just beginning. A week later their landlord, under pressure from the police, evicted them, and in October officials from surrounding Leflore County played their most powerful card. They announced that in the coming winter they would withdraw from the federal food program which distributed surplus food to the county's poor, 98 percent of whom were black and depended on the program to get through the winter when no work was available.[18]

SNCC's answer was to press on with voter registration and to fight back with a food program of its own. In December two Michigan State students, Ivanhoe Donaldson and Ben Taylor, were arrested when they tried to bring a truckload of food and clothing to Greenwood; but as the news of Greenwood's action spread nationwide, there was no way the county could stop food from coming in. In New York singer Harry Belafonte led a relief appeal at Carnegie Hall, and in Chicago comedian Dick Gregory chartered a plane to bring several tons of food to Mississippi. On just one day in February 1963 SNCC gave away more than four tons of food in Leflore County. SNCC soon found that it now had an image in the black community of providing direct aid, not just agitation. "The food is identified in the minds of everyone," Bob Moses wrote, "as food for those who want to be free, and the minimum requirement for freedom is identified as registration to vote."[19]

SNCC's successes also heightened local opposition. In late February four black businesses in Greenwood were firebombed, and when SNCC field secretary Sam Block told reporters he believed the attacks were retaliation for SNCC's food program, he was jailed for remarks "calculated to provoke a breach of the peace." A February 25 rally brought more than a hundred protesters to the Greenwood city hall, but three days later the violence escalated again. A car carrying Bob Moses, an attorney from the Voter Education Project, and Jimmy Travis, a SNCC field secretary, was fired upon. Moses and the attorney escaped unscathed, but Travis was badly hurt and had surgery in Jackson to remove a bullet from his neck.[20]

A month later tension in Greenwood rose another notch. On March 24 SNCC's offices were burned to the ground, and on March 27, after a rally protesting the firebombing, Moses, SNCC Executive Secretary James Forman, and six other SNCC workers were arrested. In their absence other civil rights leaders, among them Medgar Evers of the Mississippi NAACP and James Farmer of CORE, came to Greenwood, and soon thereafter so did the Justice Department in the person of John Doar. Greenwood was now daily news in the *New York Times*, and the Kennedy administration was under pressure to do something about it. SNCC wanted a restraining order that would force Greenwood officials to stop their harassment and allow eligible black voters to register at the courthouse. But what SNCC got was action by the Kennedy administration that paved the way for the end of voter registration in Greenwood.

After unsuccessful efforts to convince a federal district judge to issue a temporary restraining order against Greenwood officials, the administration opted for a more cautious approach. In order to get the eight SNCC staffers out of jail, the Justice Department ordered John Doar to make a deal in which the eight would be released in exchange for the Justice Department dropping a lawsuit designed to force Greenwood officials to provide police protection at the courthouse and stop harassing blacks trying to register to vote. A similar bargain was struck to restore food relief in Greenwood. Instead of suing Leflore officials, Washington agreed to pick up the county's cost for food distribution, thus allowing county officials to insist that Washington, not they, had finally backed down. By the end of the first week in April, SNCC was in a position to resume its work in Greenwood, but, as in McComb in 1961, there was little the civil rights workers could point to as tangible gain despite enormous sacrifice on their part. For the next six months SNCC staffers continued taking people to the courthouse to register, but by election day 1963 there were just fifty new black voters on the Leflore County rolls.[21]

Not until the fall of 1963 did SNCC achieve a real breakthrough in Mississippi. It came with a "Freedom Vote" in which blacks in massive numbers cast protest ballots in polling booths set up throughout the state by SNCC. The idea for the Freedom Vote grew out of talks between Bob Moses and Allard Lowenstein, a thirty-four-year-old lawyer and past president of the National Student Association. Lowenstein would later serve a term in Congress and gain national attention as the architect of the antiwar campaign to stop Lyndon Johnson from serving a second term as president, but in 1963 he was an important person in the Democratic party because of his close ties to such leading liberals as Eleanor Roosevelt and Hubert Humphrey.[22]

In 1963 Lowenstein arrived in Jackson, Mississippi, just as demonstrations over the killing of NAACP leader Medgar Evers were in progress. He was struck by how the situation in Mississippi resembled that in South Africa, which he had visited in 1959 and written about in his book *Brutal Mandate*. Lowenstein remembered the days of mourning that black South Africans had held to protest their disfranchisement, and he urged SNCC to try a similar strategy. Tim Jenkins, a Harvard law student working with SNCC that summer, found that under Mississippi law voters who believed they had been illegally prevented from registering could cast protest ballots. With Moses's encouragement, SNCC organized a thousand blacks to cast protest votes in the August Democratic primary. The results encouraged SNCC's executive committee to allow Moses to try the same strategy in the fall general elections, and in September Moses launched a second Freedom Vote campaign.[23]

The aim of the second Freedom Vote, as Moses wrote Lowenstein, was to provide the nation with dramatic proof that, contrary to what Mississippi's white politicians claimed, "if Negroes had the right to vote without fear of physical violence and other reprisals, they would do so." To assure a much larger turnout than in the August primary, polling booths were set up throughout the black community, and six thousand ballots were mailed to blacks who lived in areas where violence could be expected. At a meeting in October, Aaron Henry, president of the Mississippi NAACP, and Ed King, a white chaplain at Tougaloo College, were chosen as the Freedom Vote candidates for governor and lieutenant governor. Then, with Moses's approval, Lowenstein traveled to Stanford, where he had been a dean, and to Yale, where he had been a law student, to recruit students to help get out the black vote.[24]

Two weeks before the election, everything was in place. The SNCC staff and the students Lowenstein had recruited then fanned out across Mississippi to make sure the Freedom Vote went as planned. As expected, SNCC's efforts met with violence. Six of the Yale students were arrested within thirty-six hours of reaching Mississippi, and there were numerous beatings, including one by the police. But with the media on hand to report what was happening to the students, the violence remained limited. On election day the precautions used to make sure the Freedom Vote took place within the black community paid off. More than eighty thousand blacks cast their protest votes for Henry and King, and the media, intrigued by the idea of out-of-state students working as volunteers in a Mississippi election, gave SNCC the kind of publicity it had never received for its earlier voter registration campaigns.[25]

The success of the Freedom Vote gave SNCC new momentum. Now, instead of being limited to local campaigns, SNCC could function statewide. "There was less fear in the Negro community about taking part in civil rights," SNCC staffer Ivanhoe Donaldson observed. "For the first time since Reconstruction, Negroes held a rally on the steps of the courthouse, with their own candidates, expressing their own beliefs and ideas rather than those of the white folks."[26] But the success of the Freedom Vote also meant that SNCC now faced its biggest decision in Mississippi since Bob Moses went to McComb. Should it continue the kind of organizing it had carried on since 1961? Or should it switch to a political strategy in which Northern white college students played a key role?

The dilemma was one that success had made possible, but it was also a dilemma for which there was no painless organizational solution. An expanded Freedom Vote strategy was loaded with perils. Since coming to Mississippi, SNCC had developed a core of young black organizers on whom it could depend and who, as Bob Moses observed, "viewed themselves as some kind of unit."[27] If SNCC made the presence of white volunteers the key to its future in Mississippi, this core of young organizers would be placed in a much different position. Their influence would be diminished, and they would be forced to share control of the civil rights movement in Mississippi, to admit that by themselves blacks in Mississippi could not determine their political fate.

On the other hand, to rely on a small core of black workers was to put everything SNCC had achieved in Mississippi at risk. SNCC's Mississippi field secretaries had become heroes among blacks throughout the South and among many Northern college students as well. But if progress in Mississippi continued to be as slow as it had been from 1961 to 1963, there was every reason to believe that SNCC's Mississippi staff might soon become the guardians of a lost cause. "The staff was exhausted, and they were butting up against a stone wall, no breakthroughs for them," Bob Moses recalled. "How long could you expect them to survive working in that kind of isolation? Where was the help to come from? The civil rights organizations were not prepared to make Mississippi a focus." Indeed, by the fall of 1963 even loyal supporters were backing off. In a confidential letter of November 12, 1963, Wiley Branton, director of the Voter Education Project of the Southern Regional Council, informed Bob Moses that VEP, which since 1962 had been using foundation grants to finance voter registration throughout the South, had decided to reduce its funding of voter registration work in Mississippi to a minimum because the results could no longer justify the expenses. "Of almost equal significance to our decision," Branton concluded, "is the fact that the Justice Department has failed to get any meaningful decrees from any of the voter suits which have been filed in Mississippi and we know that until and unless favorable decrees are rendered and then vigorously imposed, we will not be able to get many people registered successfully."[28]

In mid-November 1963 the SNCC staff gathered in Greenville, Mississippi, to review its options. The meeting attracted little attention in the outside world, but it would be a turning point for SNCC and the nation. The issues raised by SNCC's staff of thirty-five blacks and seven whites at Greenville would dominate the civil rights movement for the remainder of the decade. Greenville would pave the way for the Summer Project and would at the same time demonstrate that within SNCC the debate over bringing large numbers of Northern volunteers south in 1964 was more corrosive than any threat that could be mounted by white Mississippi.

Like those who favored the Summer Project, those who opposed it began by citing the Freedom Vote. They were not at all sure that the presence of Northern students had worked to SNCC's advantage. "I question the value of the publicity we gained from the Yale students," Dona Moses declared. The opponents of the Summer Project feared that an expanded version of the Freedom Vote would, among other things, leave them face-to-face with an aroused white community and no one to help them once the summer was over. "We don't have much to gain from Negroes meeting whites," MacArthur Cotton, a former Freedom Rider and one of SNCC's first Mississippi field secretaries observed. "We've got too much to lose if they come down here and create a disturbance in two or three months, and they're gone."[29]

The political dangers of the Summer Project were, however, a greater concern for its critics than its physical dangers. Opponents of the Summer Project were prepared to keep working in a Mississippi in which, as one SNCC staffer put it, "You have to have a hunting license to shoot rabbits . . . but with Negroes it's open season—365 days a year." What they were not prepared to support was a Summer Project that jeopardized the inroads SNCC had made in Mississippi. They believed bringing a thousand whites to Mississippi for three months would put the entire Mississippi civil rights movement at risk. Dona Moses, who often disagreed with her husband at Greenville, raised the issue of students who refused to take orders from SNCC during the Freedom Vote. She focused on an especially troublesome student who insisted he was working for Allard Lowenstein, not SNCC. But the implications of her argument went much further. During the Freedom Vote whites seemed to gravitate to positions of authority, and many in SNCC worried about what would happen when whites working in Mississippi outnumbered blacks. "Up to this point you had a minority of whites working in the movement," Charlie Cobb, a former Howard University student and the originator of the 1964 Freedom School program, observed. "Now the movement is national. So what you've got now is hundreds of white people all coming South, and they can do things better than Negroes, and the question is, what do you do with them all?"[30]

Cobb did not believe that the whites who came to Mississippi aimed to take over SNCC, but he was convinced that tradition made it all too easy for blacks to turn over power to them. "I didn't say the whites take over. I said that the Negroes take the whites out of the field, then put them up in leadership roles," Cobb declared. "The tendency is for the whites to articulate the demands of Negroes to the Negro person while the Negro kids stand quietly on the side. This is not done on purpose by whites. But it is done." Cobb's fears were shared by whites on SNCC's staff. In terms almost identical to Cobb's, Mendy Samstein, a Brandeis graduate who had joined SNCC after teaching at Morehouse College in Atlanta, observed of the Summer Project, "If thousands of whites come down, there is the problem of relationships between blacks and whites. Whites convincing blacks of their rights—this entrenches the concept of white supremacy."[31]

Cobb's opposition to a Summer Project that relied on white college students did not, however, end with the issue of control. He also worried over SNCC's ability to deal with white versus black values. "Two thousand white field workers don't create the right image," one of the opponents of the Summer Project argued at Greenville, but to Cobb the problem went much deeper. "We've got the problem of American values in white society—values we're tying to change," he pointed out. If whites became dominant in the Summer Project, how could white values be challenged? Cobb wanted to know. "People can't just come down to Mississippi and say we're here to help you," he insisted. "The first consciousness that Negroes have is the thing of whites, and I don't think it helps to have the whites there."[32]

Cobb and those in SNCC who believed that civil rights "should be primarily a Negro movement" used as a positive example the postcolonial experience in Africa. They pointed out that when the colonial powers ruled, executive positions were held by whites. Now the idea was to train Africans to take over these positions. That was the path to the future in Africa, and it should be a model for SNCC as well. To develop a Summer Project that relied on white volunteers was a step backward.[33]

Given the care Bob Moses had taken to build the SNCC staff in Mississippi around a core of young black organizers who identified with one another and with working in Mississippi, the racial independence argument was a particularly powerful one. As the Greenville meeting heated up, Ivanhoe Donaldson, who had become active in SNCC in 1962 when as a student he was arrested for bringing food and clothing to welfare recipients in Leflore County, carried the argument one step further. How, he asked, could SNCC appeal to blacks with a Summer Project that depended on whites? Wouldn't blacks once again see themselves placed in a position of inferiority? "I came to SNCC, and I saw Negroes running the movement, and I felt good. These feelings might be irrational, they might be wrong, but I have to live with them. I get the feeling the way things are going in two or three years the movement will be run by white students," Donaldson declared. He did not try to put the anger he felt toward whites into a systematic argument. "You're fighting yourself all the way across the board. I find myself doing this all the time. I think one way and act the other," he confessed. But the fact that Donaldson did not try to intellectualize his feelings made them all the more powerful when he concluded, "Whites are mobile, and Negroes aren't. It's all one way. The whites are all in the Negro community, and then the whites take over leadership. . . . We're losing the one thing where the Negroes can stand first."[34]

As Charlie Cobb later acknowledged, there was an inherent contradiction in the position he and other opponents of the Summer Project took at Greenville. At a time when SNCC was demanding that the South's public institutions be desegregated, they were saying that SNCC itself should be wary of taking in more whites. "You are victims of your own rhetoric," Cobb recalled. "We [SNCC] were arguing desegregation, integration . . . the necessity for a society in which black and white did not make a difference. So you couldn't argue that you were opposed to white people coming down."[35] But logic, as Bob Moses and those who favored the Summer Project knew, would not be enough to carry the meeting at Greenville. The feelings voiced by Cobb and Donaldson were widespread in SNCC and inseparable from the pride that motivated the organization. To get beyond these feelings, SNCC needed a vision of the future more compelling than the one offered by Cobb and Donaldson.

For Bob Moses, the starting point was the impasse reached by SNCC in 1963. Cobb saw inviting whites to Mississippi in the summer of 1964 as an admission of failure. "You're conceding that you're not able to deal with the situation. I mean the reason for the 1964 Summer Project was simply that we weren't able to cope with the violence in the state." Moses did not dispute this reading of the facts, but for him they were not the whole story. There was, Moses believed, no onus on SNCC for failing to cope with racial violence in Mississippi.[36]

At Greenville Moses pointed out the areas in which SNCC was in trouble. Earlier in the year, at a SNCC staff meeting in Atlanta, Moses had admitted, "It's still not clear to my mind, even on the voting issue, that Negroes will gain the vote rapidly enough." Moses feared that the automation of the cotton crops, the poor education of blacks, and the efforts of the White Citizens Councils to move blacks out of the state were all working against SNCC. "If these programs are successful, and if they [blacks] are moved out before gaining the right to vote and you lose the population balance which you have now, then I think we will have lost," Moses observed. At Greenville Moses was not afraid to raise the same doubts. "We're not going to get people registered the way things are," he insisted. Most people on the plantations were "expendable" labor, and if the plantation owners were able to dump them as soon as they could be replaced by machines, SNCC was in trouble. "If it goes like it's going, they're going to beat us in five or six years, because the cards are stacked in their favor now," he argued.[37]

SNCC's only choice, Moses insisted, was to expand as it had done in the fall of 1963 when whites were used in the Freedom Vote and "brought a searchlight from the rest of the country with them." It was a difficult position for Moses to take, for it left him vulnerable to the charge of ignoring the needs of the staff he had recruited and playing down the problems that whites had caused. But Moses believed he had no choice. "The question of whether or not the white students coming in would take over the movement, would dominate, set back the whole process," he later concluded, "was a risk, but not as important as the risk of not being able to do anything at all."[38]

Some whites, Moses was willing to concede, had overstepped their bounds during the Freedom Vote, but SNCC's overall experience with whites in Mississippi was, he insisted, the reverse of what the opponents of the Summer Project claimed. The whites who became regular members of SNCC's Mississippi staff had done more than pull their weight. "We almost suffocated them," Moses pointed out. "They had to stay in the office. They couldn't go out on the street. They couldn't go to dances. They couldn't go to this café or that café. They were in the office. They were washing dishes. They were sweeping floors. They really were doing all the dirty work."[39]

"People say of white workers in the field they're more articulate and they're going to do the talking, and then if you get them in the office, they're better typists, and so they get into leadership positions," Moses observed. "The tone I get is that white people came in and took over, and now we're going to put them in their place." Moses understood all too well why such anger occurred, and he later conceded, "It's very hard for some of the students who have been brought up in Mississippi and are the victims of this kind of race hatred not to begin to let all of that out on the white staff." But at Greenville the only concessions Moses was prepared to make were limited, practical ones: "My position all along, and I think I've said this several times, 'You try to get as many Negroes as you can to do the job, [then] get white students in to the extent that it can't do harm to the Negro community.' . . . The type of person you have is much more important than whether he's white or not," he declared. "I'm not going to be part of an organization that says, 'No white people are going to be head of a project because they're white.' "[40]

Beyond this point there was, Moses was convinced, no room for compromise on the race issue. "My alternative is, I'll gladly leave if that's the kind of organization you want to run," he told the meeting. "Now that's your decision. If you want to run that kind of an organization, a racist organization, then count me out." But having made this declaration, Moses went on to argue that SNCC's position in the civil rights movement gave it a special opportunity to set an example of whites and blacks working together. "The one thing we can do for the country that no one else can do is to be above the race issue," he insisted. If whites were part of the Summer Project, Moses argued, it would change the way blacks saw them. "Negroes would have to take them as people. They'd learn not to let their fears and emotions get the better of them when they talk to whites," he contended. Most of all, Moses argued, SNCC needed whites because without them it was in danger of being part of a racist civil rights movement. "The only way you can break that down is to have white people working alongside you—so then it changes the whole complexion of what you're doing, so it isn't any longer Negro fighting white, it's a question of rational people against irrational people."[41]

Moses was not alone in arguing for white participation. Lawrence Guyot, a Mississippi-born SNCC field secretary, who in 1964 would head the newly formed Mississippi Freedom Democratic party, argued for an interracial Summer Project throughout the Greenville meeting. "The reason I could support it both in Moses's absence and presence was that I had learned from the Freedom Vote elections," Guyot remembered. "I had seen that the increased activity of the FBI did diminish the violence, and I was also very much aware that we were educating the volunteers." Moses also had the support of Fannie Lou Hamer. A forty-six-year-old mother of two adopted daughters, Hamer had survived the loss of her job and a terrible beating in the Winona, Mississippi, jail to become a leading figure in SNCC. She was at a point in her own life where she was, as she put it, "sick and tired of being sick and tired," and she epitomized the kind of grassroots commitment SNCC needed in order to make political inroads in Mississippi. When she spoke, it was with an authority that commanded immediate respect. At Greenville she waited until the debates were far along before offering her opinion, but when she did there was no mistaking her position on the Summer Project. "If we're going to break down this barrier of segregation, we can't segregate ourselves," she declared.[42]

In the end, Moses and those who favored a Summer Project that relied on the recruitment of Northern volunteers prevailed at Greenville, though no vote was taken. The Saturday meeting, which finished at midnight, closed instead with everyone holding hands and singing, "We Shall Overcome." But the stage had been set for SNCC to move forward in 1964 with the kind of Summer Project Bob Moses believed was necessary.

The change in SNCC's direction would, however, come

with a heavy price. Among such key Mississippi-born SNCC field secretaries as Curtis Hayes, Hollis Watkins, MacArthur Cotton, Sam Block, and Willie Peacock, there was strong opposition to a Summer Project that relied on Northern volunteers. In their eyes the debates at Greenville had misrepresented their deepest worries about the Summer Project. As they would later recall, putting the question of the Summer Project in black-white terms had obscured their fears about outsiders of *any* color dominating the civil rights movement in Mississippi.[43]

"It was not the problem of volunteers as whites but the problem of neglecting local people" that made the Summer Project strategy wrong, MacArthur Cotton later recalled. "I believed that we could spend another year going on like we were." His feelings were echoed by Curtis Hayes. "The issue of bringing in white people, bringing in lots of people was exaggerated, because folks did not have the confidence to raise the real issue—the negation of local organizers," he remembered.[44] Given all they had been through with Bob Moses, it did not occur to those who disagreed with him at Greenville to break away and form a rival group of their own. But their loyalty to SNCC and Moses did not alleviate their doubts. Those they would soon be expected to welcome—the college volunteers who had been recruited to come to Mississippi for the summer—had, sight unseen, already become threats. The seeds of civil war had been planted within the Summer Project just when closing ranks was more crucial than ever.

4

Nobody's Cannon Fodder

Getting whites to come to Mississippi in 1964 was one
problem that never occurred to the SNCC staff meeting in
Greenville. Bob Moses spoke about bringing in as many as
two thousand volunteers for the summer; others spoke of
twice that number. SNCC was right to feel so confident about
its power to recruit college students. The reasons that made it
dangerous to come to Mississippi for the summer were the
same reasons that made volunteers want to go there. As far
as the volunteers were concerned, going to Mississippi was

not simply doing what was right. It was undertaking the moral equivalent of war.[1]

When the Vietnam War worsened later in the sixties, students on campus after campus fought the draft and hoped for a safe lottery number. But in the case of Mississippi, students recruited by the Summer Project saw it as essential to put their lives on the line. The volunteers consistently spoke of the SNCC field secretaries as "veterans," and in joining the veterans they saw themselves joining an ongoing war. As one volunteer wrote home, "I begin to realize that it is a war that I will enter and that the enemy is even lunatic, even driven into frenzy by his fear."[2]

The influences on the volunteers to go to Mississippi were many, but in the spring of 1964 none was more important than the changing culture of the 1960s. Three years earlier in his inaugural address, John Kennedy had fired the imagination of students throughout the country, declaring that "the torch has been passed to a new generation of Americans" and asking the nation to join him in "a struggle against the common enemies of man: tyranny, poverty, disease, and war itself." The Peace Corps epitomized the kind of public service Kennedy believed could change the world, and for the volunteers drawn to Mississippi, it seemed essential to bring such social activism home, to target, as one volunteer put it, "the general dehumanization of American life." Despite Kennedy's caution on civil rights, he had been more outspoken on the subject than any other post–World War II president. "The Mississippi Summer Project seemed the best place to commemorate him," volunteer Paul Cowan wrote. "There, by sheer main force, one might realize the promise one had sensed in the president's words." Other volunteers voiced the same sentiments. "I believe, to use the words of President Kennedy, that race has no place in American life or law," a Yale volunteer began his Summer Project application by observing. "Kennedy was assassinated, and it really spoke to me," Greenwood volunteer Margaret Aley recalled. "His words continued to ring in my ears for a long time."[3]

For many volunteers, the violence that had taken Kennedy's life seemed very much like the violence directed against blacks in Mississippi. In both cases, they believed it had its source in the kind of irrational hatred that Kennedy challenged in the summer before his death in the televised civil rights speech he delivered on the day when black students entered the University of Alabama despite Governor George Wallace's efforts to block their admittance. "The heart of the question is whether all Americans are to be afforded equal rights and equal opportunities, whether we are going to treat our fellow Americans as we want to be treated," Kennedy insisted. "Are we to say to the world, and much more importantly to each other, that this is the land of the free except for the Negroes; that we have no second-class citizens except Negroes; that we have no class or caste system, no ghettos, no master race, except with respect to Negroes?" Then, in language that went to the heart of the volunteers' situation, the president warned, "Those who do nothing are inviting shame as well as violence. Those who act boldly are recognizing right as well as reality."[4]

In Kennedy's words and in civil rights legislation the volunteers found, above all else, a commitment to challenging the status quo in the name of a higher patriotism. Kennedy's example allowed the volunteers to insist both on their love of country and their obligation to fight for racial change in Mississippi. As volunteer Pat Vail put it, "I took very seriously Kennedy's 'Ask what you can do for your country' and the notion that we owe something back for what we were given." Unlike the student activists of the late 1960s, the volunteers of 1964 saw no reason to describe America as *Amerika*. They regarded themselves as part of a mainstream tradition, believing, as one volunteer wrote just before leaving for Mississippi, "This whole country needs changing so that everyone can live a life in which he is able to realize his full capacities as a human being."[5]

Looking around them, the volunteers saw social action as the way of the future. As the example of Michael Harrington showed, one did not need to be a president or a politician in order to practice activism effectively. Harrington, whose best-selling book *The Other America* had been read by Kennedy and was on the reading list given to all the volunteers, made the link between social activism and privilege seem as natural as the link between social success and privilege. *The Other America* went everywhere the volunteers went, even to jail. Like Kennedy, Harrington seemed to embody his beliefs. After leaving Yale Law School he came to know poverty firsthand through his participation in Dorothy Day's Catholic Worker movement on the Lower East Side of New York. When he spoke of abolishing poverty, he did so in terms of creating a new spirit in America. In *The Other America* Harrington pointed to the existence of an invisible country of between forty and fifty million people living in poverty and neglect, then insisted that changing that invisible America was a matter of will. "I work on the assumption that cannot be proved by government figures or even documented by impressions of the other America," Harrington wrote. "It is an ethical proposition, and it can be simply stated: In a nation with a technology that could provide every citizen with a decent life, it is an outrage and a scandal that there should be such social misery."[6]

Harrington had no doubt that the poverty he had seen could be ended. The nation, he argued, need not choose between guns and butter. The uniqueness of American poverty in the 1960s was that it "continued while the majority of the nation talked of itself as being 'affluent' and worried about neurosis in the suburbs." What made Harrington's kind of thinking so appealing to the volunteers was that it gave people like them a clear role to play in changing the country.

In *The Other America* Harrington talked about his own arrest for civil rights activity and the relationship of civil rights legislation to any campaign to end poverty. In particular he stressed the need for middle-class Americans to become politically involved. The poor, Harrington contended, were caught in a vicious circle that could be broken only if those who were better off rallied to their side. "I want to tell every well-fed and optimistic American that it is intolerable that so many millions should be maimed in body and spirit when it is not necessary that they should be," he wrote. "My standard of comparison is not how much worse things used to be. It is how much better they could be if only we were stirred."[7]

The students who joined the Summer Project had no doubt they were among the "we" who could make things better. When Harrington asked, "How long shall we ignore this undeveloped nation in our midst? How long shall we look the other way while our fellow human beings suffer?" the Summer Project volunteers heard a call for action that justified their own engagement. It seemed only natural for a concerned Summer Project volunteer to write on his application, "I want to work in Mississippi because I feel it is my duty as an American to end all racial oppression in this country." As another volunteer observed during his training session, "I'm going because the worst thing after burning churches and murdering children is keeping silent."[8]

Finally, the volunteers had before them the example of Martin Luther King. While to many of SNCC's front-line veterans King's piety made him "de Lawd," the Martin Luther King whom the volunteers knew from television coverage of his speeches and arrests was a man who made their own involvement in the Summer Project seem like the fulfillment of an obligation. The hero of the Montgomery bus boycott of 1955–1956 and the son of an Atlanta preacher, King had been accused, as the volunteers would be in 1964, of being an intruder in local politics. In his famous 1963

"Letter from Birmingham Jail," King answered his Southern critics, eight Alabama clergymen, with a reply that not only defended his actions but those of anyone accused of being an intruder in civil rights. "I am in Birmingham because injustice is here," King wrote. "I cannot sit idly by in Atlanta and not be concerned about what happens in Birmingham. Injustice anywhere is a threat to justice everywhere. We are caught in an inescapable network of mutuality, tied in a single garment of destiny . . . . Anyone who lives inside the United States can never be considered an outsider anywhere within its bounds."[9]

The blame for the tension in Birmingham rested, King argued, with those in the South who defended segregation and refused to change. He and the Southern Christian Leadership Conference were dramatizing the issue of segregation so that it could no longer be ignored. It was the kind of logic to which the volunteers were naturally responsive. "I no longer can escape the tension, the spirit, the anxiety that fills my heart and mind concerning the movement in the South," a volunteer wrote on his Summer Project application. Another wrote home, "I cannot agree with that 'sympathetic' American who from his 'safe' and carefully maintained distance says that we must slow up, that we must not push. I suspect this attitude, as I suspect that part of it which I see in myself." What made King's message especially appealing to the volunteers was the role it held out for them—one of reconciliation. King's confrontations rested on the supposition that when violence was met with forgiving love, not only could unjust laws be changed but so could the people responsible for them. "We will match your capacity to inflict suffering with our capacity to endure suffering. We will meet your physical force with our soul force," King had declared. "And in winning our freedom we will so appeal to your heart and conscience that we will win you in the process."[10]

How seriously the volunteers took King's view of the

future can be seen in how often their letters home read like miniature sermons rather than the writing of sons and daughters to their parents. It is not unusual to find a volunteer defending his decision to join the Summer Project by insisting, "Here is an organized program through which we can use our skills and our lives to bring some measure of justice, maybe even love, to this state and the rest of the country." Even volunteers who were not religious found themselves seeing a commitment to nonviolence in a new light. "When I came, I thought that M. L. King and his 'love your enemy' was a lot of Christian mysticism," a volunteer wrote from the Summer Project training session. "Now I can see it as a force and support, helping those who understand it. It makes me think that maybe I can take what is coming this summer."[11]

History would accentuate the differences between Kennedy, Harrington, and King. But in 1964 it was their similarities that caught the attention of the Summer Project volunteers. It was one thing for Bob Dylan in a song like "Blowin' in the Wind" to ask, "How many years can some people exist before they're allowed to be free? How many times can a man turn his head and pretend he just doesn't see?" It was very different for Kennedy, Harrington, and King to ask and answer the same questions. They provided a security and a sense of historical perspective that a peer like Bob Dylan could not.

For the volunteers, the idea of challenging Mississippi in the name of a fundamental Americanism was crucial. They did not see themselves going to Mississippi in order to turn the South into a racial utopia but in order to bring Mississippi into step with the laws of the land. As volunteer Pam Parker put it, "Mississippi was an anachronism to the basic values of the country." Barney Frank, in 1964 a Harvard graduate student and later a congressman from Massachusetts, described the volunteers' commitment as one of "chastened idealism." Frank's comment reflects how deeply rooted in tradition was the volunteers' idealism. The median income of their families was 50 percent higher than the national average, and they came from the most prestigious colleges and universities in the country—where the Summer Project organizers had deliberately recruited. In contrast to the student activists of the late 1960s, the volunteers did not believe they needed to disavow their middle-class backgrounds in order to prove their political sincerity. When they spoke of their admiration for the Summer Project staff, it was because of the staff's bravery in insisting that Mississippi grant blacks their basic constitutional rights. As one volunteer wrote, "They are taking on a state and perhaps a nation which they think has violated the fundamental rights of man. They have acted when few others would. They are speaking about a festering sore in this nation."[12]

When the volunteers described the manner in which they should go into Mississippi, it was not as an army on a crusade but as an army defending the values on which the survival of the country depended. "We should not go into Mississippi the way America went into World War I—with empty idealism and slogans about making the world safe for democracy," Holly Springs volunteer Frank Cieciorka wrote. "Rather we should approach it as Americans approached World War II—there is a dirty job to do, and we have to do it. We do not need any high-sounding slogans. We have plenty of them in the Declaration of Independence, the Constitution, and the Pledge of Allegiance."[13]

This kind of political faith in what America stood for gave the volunteers their fervor. They found no way they could hold the views they had been taught at home and in school without acting on them. As volunteer Robbie Osman recalled, "It was not enough just to be right or to have the right analysis or to uphold the right way." Inaction was not only a betrayal of the values that the volunteers saw epitomized by a John Kennedy or a Martin Luther King, it was a betrayal of themselves. In their letters home the volunteers constantly returned to the idea that they were in jeopardy if they did *not* go to Mississippi. "Concerning the 'practicality' of such a venture: nothing could be more 'lucrative,' or 'profitable,' than teaching in Mississippi this summer. . . . I do not want to spend my life in the pursuit and enjoyment of comfort and security," Bret Breneman wrote to his parents. "It is all ultimately selfish: I 'save' myself by commiting myself to the concerns of other men."[14]

To hesitate about going to Mississippi was, moreover, to lose an opportunity that might never come again. Frank Roosevelt's feeling of being "part of history in the making" was one shared by most volunteers. "I sense somehow that I am at a crucial moment in my life and that to return home where everything is secure and made for me would be to choose a kind of death," Bret Breneman declared. A Southern volunteer put the same sentiments in even more dramatic language. "I'm involved in this for my own freedom," he observed. "We have to build a new South, a South ruled by law, democracy, and humanity. I couldn't not have come."[15]

The volunteers were convinced that adults who said they supported the civil rights movement but refused to act on their convictions were hypocrites. "What's dangerous is closing our eyes like we all do most of the time and hoping we'll never see the dangers," a Batesville volunteer wrote. "I do hope that when I'm old, and this struggle, if it is to be won, is won, all of us, and everyone we touch or even brush by, will live in a more gutsy, moment-to-moment, existential fashion, whether for love or for hate, for creation or for destruction." In the same spirit a volunteer just beginning her Summer Project orientation asked her parents to accept her decision to go south even though they opposed the decision. "Convictions are worthless in themselves. In fact, if they don't become actions, they are worse than worthless—they become a force of evil in themselves. You can't run from a broadened awareness," she wrote. "If you try, it follows you in your conscience, or you become a self-deceiving person who has numbed some of his humanness. I think you have to live to the fullest extent to which you have gained an insight or you are less than the human being you are capable of being."[16]

In his autobiographical *The Making of an Un-American*, Paul Cowan recalls overhearing a telephone conversation between a volunteer and her mother that ended with the volunteer screaming, "If someone in Nazi Germany had done what we're doing, then your brother would still be alive." The specific conversation was one that only a Jewish volunteer could have had, but the thinking behind it was pervasive. The volunteers believed that Mississippi blacks faced a living death unless people like themselves took their side and refused to be "good Germans." "It was going to war. It was World War II," Tacoma volunteer Dennis Flannigan recalled. "It was going down to fight Nazis."[17]

Some volunteers were quick to acknowledge that guilt had played a role in their decision to join the Summer Project. "As to why we're going down, if anyone gave a simple answer, I'd be suspicious," observed Sam Walker, a University of Michigan senior. "Part is the American dream, you know, and part is shame. I feel a very real sense of shame." But the volunteers who expressed such feelings did not do so in order to dwell on them or to psychologize their reasons for going south. They were aware that through no act of their own they were privileged, and they believed that the only way to make sure they did not exploit that privilege was to side with those who had been denied the rights they took for granted. "It was our Spain," Marshall Ganz, thinking of the reaction of his parents' generation to the Spanish Civil War, recalled. For others the alternative to not going seemed too dreadful to contemplate. "It is less a question of choice for me than a reasonable and inevitable commitment to an action for which I find no alternative," a Clark University student wrote. A volunteer from Colgate confessed, "For me, not to help would be to deny that I am a Christian, least of all a human being and an American."[18]

"They are nobody's cannon fodder. I have never heard more honest talk among leaders and followers," Harvard staff psychologist Robert Coles, who would accompany the volunteers into Mississippi, wrote after meeting with them in June. "What I find impressive about them is that they are not yet jaded and paralyzed. Their heads may face future gunshot, but at least they do not carry their intelligence and knowledge like a millstone around their necks." Coles's assessment reflected the volunteers' own confidence in the rightness of their action. It omitted, however, the one shock for which the volunteers had not prepared themselves—doubt on the part of the Summer Project's veteran organizers. The volunteers had steeled themselves to be hated by white Mississippians, and they had faced up to their parents' fears. But in an America where blacks were just 2.9 percent of the college population, most volunteers had had little personal contact with blacks. In committing themselves to going to Mississippi, it had not occurred to them that within the SNCC itself they would find serious concerns about their motives and the wisdom of bringing an army of whites into the Deep South.[19]

5

Open the Eyes
of the Nation

"Some of you will be arrested, some of you will be beaten, and some of you may lose your lives." It was a warning that would be repeated again and again during the orientation sessions for the Mississippi Summer Project. The Summer Project staff wanted to make sure the volunteers who answered their call to come to Mississippi knew the risks they were taking. The staff were not the only ones issuing warnings. FBI Director J. Edgar Hoover, no friend of the civil rights movement, was also anxious for the volunteers to understand the danger they faced. "We most certainly do not and will not give protection to civil rights workers," Hoover declared. "The FBI is not a police organization. It is purely an investigative organization, and the protection of individual citizens, either natives of the state or coming into the state, is a matter for the local authorities."[1]

In Hoover's case the motives behind his warning were transparent. He did not want the FBI held responsible for trouble during the Summer Project. The volunteers could see where they stood in his eyes and how his warning was sure to give comfort to everyone in Mississippi who opposed their coming. The Summer Project staff's warning was another matter. It was one more reason for the volunteers to think of their orientation as basic training and to trust the Summer Project organizers. "This must be the most relentlessly honest political movement in the world," volunteer Gene Nelson wrote of the staff's willingness to acknowledge the dangers that lay ahead.[2]

There were, however, limits on what the Summer Project organizers were prepared to reveal to the volunteers or to a public initially unsure of the need for a Summer Project.[3] At SNCC's final staff meeting before the start of the project, Mississippi field secretary Doug Harris argued, "Deeper than the question of danger is that of race relations. One of our goals is having Northerners face our real attitudes." But it was difficult, even embarrassing, for Summer Project organizers to be completely candid with the volunteers when their own internal arguments were unresolved.[4]

As June began the Summer Project opponents remained convinced that a massive influx of whites into Mississippi would bring disaster. To make matters worse, they felt they had been excluded from the project's decision-making process. Charlie Cobb, who had dropped out of Howard to become a full-time SNCC worker in Mississippi, recalled that after Greenville, "All the other discussions about the

Mississippi Summer Project were really not happening where most of the Mississippi people were." His views were echoed by other Mississippi workers. "We stood out like a sore thumb," Sam Block said of himself and the opponents of the Summer Project. "We had this big Summer Project being organized from without," Curtis Hayes remembered with sadness. "It wasn't the Mississippi people deciding."[5]

The Summer Project opponents had reason to feel slighted. If they had read the September 7, 1963, *San Francisco Chronicle*, they would have found an interview with John Lewis in which he spoke of SNCC initiating a Summer Project in Mississippi of such magnitude that "the Federal Government will have to take over the State."[6] But the Summer Project Lewis envisioned was not one that SNCC had come even close to approving. After the Greenville meeting in November, SNCC's next discussion of the Summer Project did not occur until an executive committee meeting in Atlanta in late December.

At that meeting the objections raised at Greenville were raised again, and once again went unresolved. Rather than falling into bitter discussion, the executive committee passed a proposal by Marion Barry, its first chairman and the future mayor of Washington, which read, "During the presidential year of 1964, SNCC intends to obtain the right for all citizens of Mississippi to vote, using as many people as necessary to obtain that end." What allowed Barry's motion to pass was its ambiguity. It did not require the SNCC staff to choose between a controlled experiment limited to a hundred volunteers and a program, now being called the "saturation proposal," that would bring a thousand or more volunteers to Mississippi.[7]

A month later SNCC was still debating whether the Summer Project should use a hundred or a thousand volunteers. A January 24 meeting in Hattiesburg was another rerun of Greenville. Presided over by SNCC Executive Secretary James Forman, the meeting did little to reassure those who believed, as Mississippi field secretary George Greene charged, "The staff has been forced into the Summer Project." Opponents of the project like Frank Smith continued to insist that SNCC was turning to white students because of a pattern of "not recruiting and developing state talent." Even SNCC staffers who favored an all-out Summer Project acknowledged that SNCC was not prepared to handle a thousand new volunteers.[8]

For Bob Moses, January was, however, a turning point. At SNCC's December executive committee meeting in Atlanta, Moses had made a cautiously restrained case for the Summer Project, but by the end of January he was back to his Greenville stance. What changed Moses was the murder of Lewis Allen, an Amite County logger who had witnessed the 1961 shooting of Herbert Lee by E. H. Hurst. After the shooting of Lee was ruled a justifiable homicide, Allen offered to come forward and tell his version of the story—Hurst had simply shot Lee in a rage—if the federal government would offer him protection. The FBI interviewed Allen, but when the Justice Department refused to indict Hurst, Allen was put in the worst possible position. His willingness to talk was known to everyone in Amite County, but there was nothing the federal government could do to help him. For Moses, who in 1962 had written to John Doar saying of Allen, "They are after him in Amite," Allen's murder in January 1964 was a devastating blow. It meant that after three years of organizing it was still open season on anyone who helped SNCC. "We had come full circle," Moses concluded. He was now prepared to push as hard as possible for a Summer Project that would bring enough white volunteers to Mississippi to protect SNCC's field secretaries and anyone who sided with them.[9]

Moses's commitment to such a Summer Project, added to the support it already had, was enough to initiate plans to bring a thousand volunteers to Mississippi. But Moses could not resolve the nagging doubts that remained among the opponents of the Summer Project. When the SNCC staff gathered in Atlanta a few days before the start of orientation for the Summer Project, the debate was voiced anew.

"Our problems are similar to those of a person moving from a small town to a large urban community: he no longer knows the people around him as well," James Forman observed as the June meeting began. But with the volunteers' orientation sessions only days away, Forman's soothing words could not lessen the tensions the SNCC staff was feeling. "The conversation sounds as though this is the first discussion of white involvement," the normally soft-spoken Ella Baker, one of SNCC's founders, complained. "Perhaps we have an inflated ego? Are we prepared to take the revolution one step further?" she asked. Her question was one which the SNCC staff was not prepared to answer collectively, and as the meeting ended, it was Dona Moses, one of the early opponents of the Summer Project, who summed up SNCC's internal divisions. "We must set the tone at the Oxford orientation session for the relationship between black and white workers," she insisted. Then she conceded, as much in sadness as in anger, "We began these discussions in Greenville in November, but the talk was cut off. We didn't really grapple with the problems because people were ashamed of admitting their feelings. When the talk becomes moralistic, it gets shut off."[10]

The difference between fighting over these issues in November and in June was that in June, with the media everywhere, open fights were risky. In their appeals to Northern supporters, the Summer Project staff had played up the past contributions of white students. "Last November, college students came down from Stanford and Yale, and with their help, in a three-day weekend, we were able to turn out some 82,000 votes in our own Freedom Election," SNCC field secretary Ivanhoe Donaldson told contributors at a New York fund-raising meeting in April. "The willingness of the students to come to Mississippi led to the development of the program for this summer." Now that the summer was starting, an organizer like Donaldson could not, despite his misgivings, turn around and say publicly that white volunteers might be a menace to the civil rights movement in Mississippi.[11]

As the orientation sessions began, the Summer Project organizers thus found themselves trying to find a way to be honest and at the same time keep a lid on the issues that mattered most to them. The most volatile of these issues, as Greenville showed, was the anger so many black organizers felt toward whites. There was no way an organizer, especially one who had grown up in Mississippi, could suddenly put aside a lifetime of memories just because he was part of the civil rights movement. "We're going through a big thing right now in terms of the attitude of the Negro staff toward the white staff," Bob Moses observed months before the Summer Project began. "It's very hard for some of the students who have been brought up in Mississippi and are the victims of this kind of race hatred not to begin to let all of that out on the white staff." But how did a SNCC worker acknowledge such feelings in June, especially when it was not clear they could be controlled? As Hollis Watkins, one of the young Mississippi field secretaries Bob Moses had brought into SNCC, observed just before the volunteers' orientation began, "We don't know what will happen with whites coming into the state. Neither do we know our own feelings and hatred of whites."[12]

Equally tough was the issue of white martyrdom. By bringing whites into Mississippi the Summer Project was openly responding to the country's indifference to the killing of Southern blacks. "When you come south, you bring with you the concern of the country—because the people of the country don't identify with Negroes," Bob Moses told the volunteers during their training sessions. "Now the federal government is concerned: there will be more protection for us, and hopefully for the Negroes who live there." But there was a thin line between knowing the galvanizing effect a white death would have on public opinion and hoping the summer would produce a white martyr. "It is a dreadful thing to say, but it needs saying. The organizers who sent these young people into Mississippi must have wanted, even hoped for martyrs," columnist Joseph Alsop charged in the *Washington Post*. Such accusations stung Bob Moses, and during orientation he made a special point of reminding the volunteers that he and the project staff would be facing the same dangers as they. "I justify myself because I'm taking the same risks myself, and I'm not asking other people to do things I'm not willing to do," he declared.[13]

Moses's claim could be echoed by all of SNCC's Mississippi field secretaries, but it did not allay their sensitivity to the kind of charge Alsop had leveled. At SNCC's last meeting before the Summer Project orientation, Ruby Doris Robinson, who would later become SNCC's executive secretary, observed, "We know that the Summer Project was conceived with the idea that there would be bloodshed, but what does it mean to say that violence will be brought to the doorstep of the White House?" In a similar vein, veteran Mississippi organizer Charles McLaurin, noting SNCC's desire to have the Summer Project "open the eyes of the nation," asked, "If the latter is our goal, perhaps we should send whites into new communities where violence will occur." All of SNCC's black staffers knew how exposed their work in Mississippi left them, and it was easy for them to calculate the benefits a white death would bring. But when they found themselves thinking that a white death would provide them with a political shortcut, they had, they knew, begun in some terrible way to adopt the ruthlessness of those they were fighting.[14]

The implications raised by the white martyrdom issue, like those raised by the suspicion of reverse racism, could not be easily confined. Particularly among SNCC's Mississippi staff, thinking about white martyrdom was inseparable from thinking about the kind of racial self-hatred that said a white life was more precious than a black life. Bob Moses had no trouble insisting that SNCC could not go it alone and win in Mississippi. As far as he was concerned, opening up the civil rights movement to whites was not just a confession of fallibility, it was an opportunity to make the civil rights movement multiracial. But for those black SNCC field secretaries who did not share Moses's view of the future, the Summer Project was a step backward, capitalizing on what SNCC veteran Mary King, who, with Julian Bond, handled most of the Summer Project press releases, called "the double standard and racism of the news media." Such a strategy, Summer Project opponents felt, furthered black self-hatred. In their eyes SNCC was doing more than accepting the idea that in white America only white suffering mattered. It was building a vital part of the Summer Project around the belief that the same whites who would be indifferent to more black deaths in white Mississippi would be touched if *white* students were killed.[15]

The Summer Project staff also worried about the kinds of volunteers who had been recruited. In its first memo to accepted volunteers, the project committee pointedly warned that it reserved the right to "deselect" any summer worker. Behind the warning lay the committee's awareness that its volunteer selection process had been highly uneven. In April the committee had sent its interviewers a memo entitled, "Guidelines for Interviewing," stressing that prospective volunteers should be told that their "role would be a stopgap one" which obliged them "to *work with* local leadership, not to overwhelm it." "A student who seems determined to carve his own niche, win publicity and glory when he returns home, can only have harmful effects on the Mississippi program," the committee wrote. But finding that harmful student ahead of time was not always easy.[16]

A Wesleyan University panel, headed by Professor John Maguire, a former Freedom Rider, eliminated ten of the nineteen candidates it interviewed, and in Boston, where there was great interest in the Summer Project, interviews often lasted an hour. But volunteers from smaller cities and colleges, especially in the Midwest, often were not interviewed at all, or, just as serious, the results of interviews were frequently not sent on to those charged with making final decisions. The problems in the interview process were reflected in a letter sent to SNCC recruiters in early May by Dorothy Zellner, a SNCC staffer interviewing out of Boston. "As I understand it," Zellner wrote in a letter mailed with SNCC's approval, "very few cities or schools are conducting interviews, or if they have, very few results of these interviews are getting down to Jackson." On the eve of its orientation sessions, the Summer Project staff thus had no idea if the volunteers it had recruited could stand up to the pressures of Mississippi. "Almost all of us felt ambivalence, in my case a feeling of dread, at the thought of the arrival of one thousand innocents," Mary King later wrote in her memoir, *Freedom Song.* "We wondered to ourselves, How do we know they are coming for the right reasons? Some of the staff openly resented the volunteers and thought they would not be pure enough. Others feared that lives would be lost."[17]

In the case of SNCC's Mississippi veterans, the lives they thought might be lost included their own. "It was easy for us to conceal ourselves in the black community, but there was no way they could," Willie Peacock remembered thinking. White volunteers, Peacock believed, were sure to make blacks like him an easier target. His thoughts were echoed by Charlie Cobb, who on the eve of the Summer Project warned, "There are certain areas where whites cannot work.

Having whites in some areas would limit the mobility of Negro workers because the danger would be so increased."[18]

The anxieties of the Summer Project staff were reflected in the two week-long orientation sessions held in June at Western College for Women in Oxford, Ohio. The sessions were crammed with more history, more role-playing, more warnings about the dangers that lay ahead than the volunteers could begin to absorb. The notes taken by the volunteers during their orientation read like a year-long college course on the South. The sessions included lectures from SNCC staffers Bob Moses, James Forman, and Stokely Carmichael as well as from such movement figures as Bayard Rustin, Ed King, and Aaron Henry. Even the Justice Department was included in the curriculum. On Friday of each week John Doar, the first assistant attorney general for civil rights, came from Washington to discuss the limited role the federal government could be expected to take in Mississippi over the summer.[19]

For most of the more than five hundred volunteers who came to Ohio, the heart of orientation was not, however, the lectures or the role-playing sessions. Crucial for them was their personal contact with the Summer Project staff. Gathering at Oxford the volunteers looked like the "innocents" Mary King imagined they would be. In contrast to the SNCC field secretaries in their blue jeans and work shirts, the volunteers—the boys in khaki pants and button-down shirts, the girls in denim skirts and bright blouses—seemed to bring the suburbs with them. As the mother of a volunteer wrote of her daughter's first day at Oxford, "It looked like a gay college weekend. All day buses spilled out youngsters with sleeping bags and guitars."[20]

Despite their fears of what lay ahead, the volunteers

reached Oxford in a mood of exhilaration. They were, they believed, at last among "friends" who thought as they did and who would not continually be asking them to explain why they were going to Mississippi. "It's wonderful to live with three hundred people who feel the same way," Karol Nelson wrote as her orientation week began. Margaret Aley noted, "Somehow I feel like I've found something I've been looking for for a long time. I feel like I've finally come home." The presence of the media added to the excitement. Friends and parents might have doubts about the Summer Project, but clearly reporters were taking it seriously. "They followed us into classrooms and dormitories, around the lounges, out along the paths," Sally Belfrage recalled. "They asked people to sing that song again for the American public. There was footage, yardage, mileage of every face in the place."[21]

It was still necessary to write parents, but suddenly roles had been switched. Now the volunteers were doing the reassuring and explaining. "It is very hard to answer to your attitude that if I loved you I wouldn't do this," Bonnie Guy wrote to her parents. "I can only hope you have the sensitivity to understand that I can *both* love you very much and desire to go to Mississippi." Peggie Dobbie used similar words trying to comfort her parents: "I write this letter because I know you are concerned about me and because I know the best way for me to show my concern for you is to be honest. Please gain some sense of confidence and peace of mind by knowing that this training session is preparing us in the best possible way for what we will encounter in Mississippi. I think perhaps I am loving you more now than I ever have."[22]

By contrast, the arriving volunteers' attitude toward the Summer Project staff was one of hero worship. "I got to Oxford, where these legendary, mythical characters met us," Dennis Flannigan recalled. "These were the people who had been getting their asses kicked and shot. There was this awe." In the volunteers' eyes the staff stood out as models. As Radcliffe student Kathie Amatniek put it, "They were so much more wonderful and exciting than anybody I had met in college." Above all, there was the example of Bob Moses. Lisa Anderson remembered, "Bob Moses stood out for everybody. He was an incredibly strong figure. He was calm. He was effective. What he said made sense, and you wanted to do what he said should be done."[23]

Such idealization was severely tested, however, when SNCC field secretaries like Frank Smith, now a city councilman in Washington, D.C., made a point of telling the volunteers, "I grew up hating all white folks. It wasn't until a couple years ago that I learned there could be good whites, and even now I sometimes wonder." Many volunteers found their welcome at Oxford very different from what they expected. "The reception at Western College was not warm. I was surprised at how unfriendly and unextending people were," one volunteer wrote after his first day. "Right now we don't know what it is to be a Negro, and even if we did, the Negroes here would not accept us. It's the old case of having to prove ourselves. In their eyes we're rich middle or upper class whites who've taken off a summer to help the Negro." His sentiments were echoed in a letter written two days later by Bill Hodes that began, "There has been increasing tension here over our relations with the Negro staff members, especially the ones who hail from Mississippi. They are very much of an in-group because of what they have gone through together. They tend to be suspicious of us, because we are white, Northern, urban, rich, inexperienced. We are somewhat in awe of them, and conscious of our own inferiority."[24]

What separated the volunteers was how they dealt with this tension. Many saw it as the price of going to Mississippi and treated it like any encounter in which those who are new must win the approval of those who are experienced. "Us white kids are in a position we've never been in before," one volunteer noted soon after arriving. "The direction of the whole program is under Negro leadership—almost entirely. And a large part of that leadership is young people from the South—Negroes who've had experience just because they're Negroes and because they've been active in the movement. And here 'we' are, for the most part never experiencing any injustice other than, 'No, I won't let you see your exam paper.'" Other volunteers took the staff's suspicions as having nothing to do with them personally and everything to do with history. "So, there is this great reluctance and distrust, born of generations of oppression and slavery," Ellen Lake noted. "It seems that if more whites understood this—especially white liberals—race relations might be a lot less strained." Still other volunteers drew a political lesson from the anger they felt directed toward them. "I took it both as an object lesson—we ought to learn how to deal with this, and I took it to mean that the role of whites was not to lead the black movement," Heather Tobis, who in 1973 would found the Midwest Academy, a training school for organizers, recalled.[25]

Nonetheless, close to the surface in even the most easygoing volunteers were the feelings that prompted one to write home, "Intellectually, I think many of us whites can understand the Negroes' resentment but emotionally we want to be 'accepted' at face value. We want this acceptance because this is part of our reason for going down South, i.e., the basic worth of the individual." In her novel *Civil Wars*, which begins with an account of the Summer Project, Rosellen Brown describes a situation in which Jesse Carll, a young volunteer from New York City, loses her patience with a Summer Project staffer who has pushed her beyond endurance. "One night she had it out with a young woman named Edith Eddy, who had a huge voice, church grown, who loved to use it to humiliate the volunteers," Brown writes. "Jesse marched over to her at dinner one night—her whole table watched the encounter—and accused Edith of wanting it both ways: we came to help, invited, and we are repulsed, derided, laughed at. What the hell, she demanded, is going on here? Are we going to risk our lives or are we not?" The anger expressed by Brown's fictional Jesse Carll was never so dramatically stated at Oxford, but it was certainly felt by many volunteers.[26]

"It was the most depressing week of my life. Just the worst thing I ever went through," a California student observed. "All they did for eleven hours a day was talk about how prejudiced we were. The staff wouldn't talk to us, it was like they despised us." Even Sally Belfrage, one of the most sensitive chroniclers of the Summer Project, found her confidence shaken by the questioning she faced during orientation. "Over and over in Ohio they had told us that we were all the victims of the very prejudice we fought. How could this be so? We were forced to examine ourselves for symptoms of the disease," Belfrage wrote in her *Freedom Summer*. "It humbled, if not humiliated, one to realize that *finally, they will never accept me*. And this raised the question: Why, then, am I here? If they're not grateful for my help, if we are supposed to be struggling for brotherhood and can't even find it among ourselves, why am I here?"[27]

It was scarcely surprising that during both orientation sessions the volunteers and Summer Project staff ended up openly confronting each other. During the first orientation session the confrontation occurred on a Tuesday evening after the showing of a CBS news report, "Mississippi and the Fifteenth Amendment." In the report segregationist Mississippi was represented by an obese white registrar and a rabid white lawyer. The volunteers could not believe their eyes. Both the registrar and the lawyer seemed like parodies of bigots rather than dangerous foes, and instead of taking them seriously, many of the volunteers began to laugh. The laughter caused six of the Summer Project staff to leave the room, and when the lights went back on, the volunteers were met with the anger of the staffers who remained. "You should be ashamed. You could laugh at that film!" a furious staffer shouted. "Six of the SNCC field workers left this room when you laughed. They couldn't believe their ears, and neither could I. I hope by the end of the summer you will never laugh at such a film again."[28]

Later, in a meeting that lasted until two in the morning, staff and volunteers confronted each other with the anger they were feeling. It was humiliation, not laughter, that SNCC's Mississippi field secretaries had experienced in their encounters with registrars and racist lawyers, and to watch the volunteers' amusement at the film was to be insulted again. For the staff it was doubly menacing to be headed into Mississippi with allies who didn't realize that in the Deep South the most insignificant-appearing whites had power as long as they were part of the system. "If you don't get scared, pack up and get the hell out of here because we don't need any favors of people who don't know what they are doing here in the first place," a staff member told the stunned volunteers.[29]

As the evening wore on, the staff returned again and again to the same theme: they were the adults, the volunteers were the children. And the children had to understand. "We cried for you in the staff meeting, because we love you and are afraid for you. We are grown men and women, hardened fighters who have been beaten and shot at, and we cried for you," one SNCC worker declared. Then he went on to talk about his experiences in the army. "I was a good soldier in Korea. I can stick a bayonet in your back in the right spot so that you don't make a sound. I know how to use piano wire around your neck and then let you fall to the ground soft," he told the volunteers. "Don't worry when we don't have time to shake your hands, because that is not the SNCC greeting anyway. We hug and kiss you because we love you."[30]

Neither the staff nor the volunteers acted as if there was anything odd about a story that moved so quickly from civil rights to killing with a bayonet. For both groups, the details of the dialogue were far less important than the tone being established. "We all sang together, and the first time *really* together. The crisis is past, I think," volunteer Bill Hodes wrote home. Hodes was not just putting the best face on a situation that deeply shook the volunteers. What had occurred was a collective recognition by the volunteers of the staff's authority. In their letters home volunteers like Patrick Thomas had no qualms about saying, "Hopefully it is just a matter of another week or two before I become as free from Northern-white-liberal prejudices as it is possible for me to become." The meeting made such feelings public. The volunteers were forced to acknowledge that even with the best of intentions they brought a racial ignorance with them. The project staffers in turn were made the source of judgment and forgiveness. They would be the ones to say when the volunteers could be trusted, when their actions separated them from the white world they left behind.[31]

A similar confrontation during the second week occurred when Jimmy Travis, a SNCC field secretary who had been shot during the 1963 Greenwood campaign, finished a long and moving talk about the dangers of Mississippi. "It's hell in Mississippi. And you're got to realize that nobody cares," Travis told the volunteers. "I'm black. You're white. If you're going down there, you're going to be treated worse than black. Because you are supposed to be free. But I say no one is free until everyone is." The volunteers were deeply touched by Travis's words, and when he stopped speaking, they applauded. But when the applause died down, Travis was not to be seen. He had left the room through the door behind him. In the uneasy quiet that followed, a young staffer

from Mississippi told the volunteers, "You've got to understand Jimmy. He was nearly killed. It was something he had
to say. You shouldn't applaud." This time the repercussions
were not as great as those of the first week's confrontation,
but the lesson for the volunteers remained the same. The
staff, not they, would pass final judgment on their fitness as
civil rights workers. The instincts they brought with them
from college and suburbia were unequal to what lay ahead.[32]

How many such confrontations would it take to bridge
the gap between the Summer Project staff and volunteers?
Would they leave wounds that could not be healed? During
the orientation sessions at Oxford, these were not questions
that could be resolved. Many volunteers headed for Mississippi believing, as Kirsty Powell wrote, "We could have left
Oxford with a much more positive understanding of what we
were setting out to do, danger or no danger." But even if the
staff and volunteers had wanted to, they would have been
hard pressed to continue worrying over what divided them.
On Sunday June 21, as the first wave of volunteers was
arriving in Mississippi and the second was taking up residence
in Ohio, CORE's Meridian Community Center was struggling with a problem that would throw the Summer Project
into crisis: three Summer Project workers, Michael Schwerner, James Chaney, and Andrew Goodman, were missing.[33]

6

There May Be More Deaths

The disappearance of Schwerner, Chaney, and Goodman permanently changed the way the Summer Project was perceived by the nation, but as the project staff in Ohio struggled to get the story, there was little information available. On Sunday evening, June 21, Mary King at the SNCC communications office in Atlanta received a call from the CORE Community Center in Meridian reporting that Schwerner, Chaney, and Goodman had not been heard from hours after they were due back. King, as well as Summer Project workers in Meridian and Jackson, then began calling all the Mississippi jails to which the three men might have been taken. But at one o'clock on Monday morning, when she telephoned the Justice Department's John Doar at his home in Washington, King still had little to report except a growing sense of dread.[1]

From their own sources the Summer Project leadership knew that on Saturday morning the three men had left Oxford for Meridian. They had wanted to be sure of arriving while it was still light, and by driving without stopping they had reached Meridian by 5:30 in the evening. After settling the volunteers who had driven with them in their housing assignments, the three then went to a movie. On Sunday they were up early to drive to Longdale in nearby Neshoba County. The trip was one that Schwerner was especially anxious to make. The previous Tuesday the Mount Zion Methodist Church in Longdale had been burned to the ground. Schwerner had persuaded the Mount Zion congregation to let the Summer Project use its church to house a Freedom School, and he wanted to let them know that neither he nor anyone associated with the Summer Project was going to allow what had happened to be forgotten.[2]

The trip to Longdale had gone as planned. The three men inspected the church ruins and visited with several members of the congregation before leaving for the return trip to Meridian at three in the afternoon. But for Mary King and the rest of the Summer Project staff, what happened after Schwerner, Chaney, and Goodman left Longdale was a mystery. On Monday morning, when Mary King phoned Andrew Goodman's family in New York City and Rita Schwerner, Michael's wife, who was still in Ohio, she had nothing concrete to tell them.[3]

For Andrew Goodman, the trip to Longdale carried with it no special fears. Three days after his disappearance his parents received a card from him postmarked Sunday P.M.

that read, "I have arrived safely in Meridian, Mississippi. This is a wonderful town and the weather is fine. I wish you were here. The people in this city are wonderful and our reception was very good." Michael Schwerner, on the other hand, knew the trip to Longdale in Neshoba County—although less than forty miles—could be risky. The law and the Klan were far more dangerous there than in Lauderdale County, where Meridian was located, and Schwerner left strict instructions for the Meridian office to begin emergency procedures if he did not return by four o'clock.[4]

With any luck, Schwerner's instructions might have saved all three men's lives. But when Summer Project workers began calling jails—logs show that the Philadelphia jail where the three men were being detained was telephoned at 5:30 Sunday afternoon—they were told that no one had seen them. It was not until Monday afternoon that the Summer Project staff finally learned that Schwerner, Chaney, and Goodman had been arrested by Neshoba County Deputy Sheriff Cecil Price and held in jail until ten o'clock Sunday night, when they were released after posting a twenty-dollar bond. Even this information was, however, suspect. It did not come from a Summer Project source but from Neshoba County Deputy Sheriff Lawrence Rainey, who told the FBI, "They were here all right. Price arrested the nigger for driving seventy miles an hour in a thirty-mile zone, and he held the other two for investigation. When they paid a twenty-dollar bond for speeding, Price told them not to hang around Philadelphia, but to be on their way."[5]

To those in the movement, the story was all too familiar. Tuesday afternoon, when the blue Ford station wagon that the three men had been driving was found burned and abandoned in the nearby Bogue Chitto swamp, the Summer Project staff was sure the worst had happened. Too many questions remained unanswered. Why had callers been told that the three men were not in the Philadelphia jail when they were? Why had Schwerner, an experienced civil rights worker, not insisted on remaining in jail until morning, when it would be safer to drive? And if the three men had left the jail at night, why had they not called Meridian on their release to report that they were all right? To make matters worse, the Bogue Chitto swamp was six miles northeast of Philadelphia—but the route back to Meridian went south. It was hard to avoid the conclusion that the last people to see the three men alive—Mississippi law officials—also had a hand in their deaths. "The kids are dead," Bob Moses told the second group of volunteers at Oxford. "When we heard the news at the beginning, I knew they were dead. When we heard they had been arrested, I knew there had been a frame-up."[6]

But this was not another Mississippi lynching that would be forgotten. Neither the federal government nor the media could ignore the disappearance of three civil rights workers twenty-four hours after their arrival in Mississippi from Ohio. Because of the Summer Project, Schwerner, Chaney, and Goodman were three young men whose disappearance aroused immediate public concern. The more one learned about their lives, moreover, the more they added up to a tableau of the civil rights movement at its best. Schwerner was a Cornell and Columbia University graduate who had given up his job as a New York City social worker to move with his wife to the small town of Meridian. Chaney was a black Mississippi high school dropout who had found new meaning and purpose in his life since joining Schwerner in CORE. Goodman was a Queens College sophomore who, rather than ask his parents for the money needed to go to Mississippi, had taken a job loading trucks at United Parcel Service.[7]

From the start the media had run stories on the Ohio orientation. Now, with the fate of three civil rights workers a national concern, rural Mississippi itself was news. Television coverage intensified, and *Life* ran a feature story in which a picture of Andrew Goodman at Oxford, Ohio, was juxtaposed with a picture of white Mississippians taunting the men searching the swamps for bodies. "Now we were finding it possible to break news stories," Mary King recalled. "We were no longer toiling. The press corps was there in Mississippi." Not realizing the sudden shift in mood, Sheriff Lawrence Rainey struck a pose of nonchalance, telling the press, "If they're missing, they just hid out somewhere trying to get a lot of publicity, I figure." His sentiments were echoed by Governor Paul Johnson, who joked to reporters, "They could be in Cuba." For a state anxious to defend its way of life, this was a public relations disaster. It was made even worse as Southern papers like the *Birmingham News* began filing stories from Philadephia that reported, "Few Mississippians, official or otherwise, seem to be doing very much active searching."[8]

Four days after Schwerner, Chaney, and Goodman were reported missing, the level of media scrutiny that Mississippi would receive over the course of the summer was made dramatically clear in a CBS news special, "The Search in Mississippi," with Walter Cronkite. In the CBS special, Mississippi officials were given a chance to make their case. Both Senator James Eastland and Governor Paul Johnson were interviewed. But in the context of events in Philadelphia and in the face of report after report from black Mississippians who had been beaten or fired from their jobs for trying to vote, nothing seemed so unconvincing as the portrait of Mississippi that Senator Eastland sought to paint when he declared, "A Negro in Mississippi is employed, makes good wages, he's prosperous, he has the finest school system in the United States for his children to attend. They're doing all right. They're happy and they're prosperous." Nor did Governor Johnson come off any better when he tried to discredit the Summer Project by characterizing the volunteers as "beatnik-type people: long beards, ringlets of hair on the back of their neck, down almost to their shoulder blades—

strict nonconformists." After the program's interviews with the mother of Andrew Goodman, with volunteers, and with Aaron Henry, head of the Mississippi NAACP, Eastland and Johnson seemed to be telling the truth only when they slipped back into their old roles and warned, as Johnson did, "We are going to see to it that law and order is maintained, and maintained Mississippi-style."

In the end it was Professor James Silver, a member of the University of Mississippi history department and author of *Mississippi: The Closed Society*, who dominated the CBS special. In direct contrast to Eastland and Johnson, Silver insisted that change would happen in Mississippi because the Summer Project had created an environment in which white Mississippi could no longer defy public opinion. "What happens in Mississippi depends, it seems to me, and always has depended, more on what the people in the rest of the country think than on what people in Mississippi think," Silver declared. It was an observation that by implication gave the media an important role to play in the civil rights movement, and as the news special drew to a close, Silver was given the final chance to speak. "Ten years from now there's no question about all Mississippians having what we consider basic American rights," he predicted. "Mississippi must conform. It can no longer subvert the Constitution of the United States."[9]

The disappearance of the three civil rights workers also made action imperative for Lyndon Johnson. There was no way the president could stand aside and let matters take care of themselves when three days after the disappearance of Schwerner, Chaney, and Goodman Mississippi Governor Johnson declared, "If I were a parent, I would discourage my child from participating in this movement because of the tragic consequences that could be faced by any youngster, coming into the jaws of a situation that they knew nothing whatsoever about." If the president failed to intervene in

Mississippi, he would invite more killing in the coming months. Johnson, the president and Southerner, knew that Johnson, the governor and Southerner, would exploit any hesitancy on the part of the federal government.[10]

The president's first step was to focus federal resources on Mississippi. Sailors from the naval air station in Meridian were sent to help search the Bogue Chitto swamp for the bodies of the three civil rights workers. The parents of Michael Schwerner and Andrew Goodman were given a White House meeting when they came to Washington. Former Central Intelligence Agency chief Allen Dulles was sent to Mississippi to meet the officials there. Like his meeting with the grieving parents, the president's initial moves were in large measure symbolic. But the symbolism, which was followed by what the Justice Department's John Doar later described as the FBI's "full court press" against the Klan in Mississippi, had a point. The president was sending an unmistakable message: his administration would not trust Mississippi officials to clear up a suspected murder and kidnaping fostered by the Mississippi racial climate. Mississippi officials were shocked when on July 10 FBI Director J. Edgar Hoover personally went to Jackson to open the Bureau's new office there. But among the president's closest advisers there was no surprise. Years later Bill Moyers, a Johnson aide and confidant, recalled the meeting in which the president made it clear to Hoover that unless he went to Mississippi there would be a new FBI director—liberal Richard Goodwin, a former law clerk to Supreme Court Justice Felix Frankfurter and a key Johnson speech writer.[11]

The disappearance of Schwerner, Chaney, and Goodman also made the time right, the president believed, for passage of the civil rights bill that had been moving slowly through Congress since John Kennedy proposed it a year earlier. Within civil rights circles there had been serious doubts about Johnson's position. "With John F. Kennedy dead, the civil rights movement in America must now consider the probability of a major setback in the progress it has made during his administration," a November 25, 1963, COFO newsletter observed. Such fears were understandable, but they failed to imagine what Johnson would be like as president. On February 10, 1964, Kennedy's civil rights bill passed the House of Representatives by a vote of 290 to 130, and on June 19, ten days after the end of a record-breaking seventy-five-day filibuster which lasted 534 hours, the Senate passed its version of the Civil Rights Act 73 to 27. Now the president began putting pressure on Congress to reach agreement on a bill that he could sign no later than July 4. The president would later tell Bill Moyers, "I think we just delivered the South to the Republican Party for a long time to come." But in the wake of the Schwerner, Chaney, and Goodman disappearance, the president was most worried about being overtaken by events in the present.[12]

On July 2, two days ahead of schedule, the president got the civil rights bill he wanted. Five hours later, in a White House signing ceremony timed to coincide with the evening television news, the president addressed the nation. A year later, in proposing the Voting Rights Act of 1965, the president would adopt the language of the civil rights movement—"We shall overcome," he would promise. But this time too there was no mistaking the moral fervor of the president's language. "One hundred and eighty-eight years ago this week a small band of valiant men began a long struggle for freedom," the president told the nation. "Now our generation of Americans has been called on to continue the unending search for justice within our own borders." To anyone listening at all carefully, it was clear that the president was comparing the work of the Founding Fathers with that of the civil rights movement. He did not have to mention the Mississippi Summer Project by name for his television audience to see the linkage. By his timing, by his insistence that the new Civil Rights Act gave him the authority to act in local situations "when others cannot or will not do the job," the president was laying out his course. His administration would not let the disappearance of Schwerner, Chaney, and Goodman be forgotten.[13]

All along the Summer Project organizers had said the country would react with shock if a white volunteer were killed in Mississippi, so there was no way they could claim surprise at the response of the media and the Johnson administration to the disappearance of Schwerner, Chaney, and Goodman. It was nonetheless painful to see their own predictions so thoroughly borne out. "It is a shame national concern is aroused only after two white boys are missing," SNCC chairman John Lewis observed. Rita Schwerner was far more bitter. "We all know that the search with hundreds of sailors is because my husband and Andrew Goodman are white," she declared. "If only Chaney was involved, nothing would have been done."[14]

There was, however, no time for the Summer Project organizers to dwell on their own pained feelings. In addition to bringing attention to the project, the disappearance of the three men also brought it a unity which the Ohio orientation had not by itself generated. The potential civil war brewing inside the Summer Project suddenly took on a new perspective. Survival now became the overwhelming issue for staff and volunteers.

From the start, part of the appeal of the Summer Project was the risk it involved. Volunteers Paul and Rachel Cowan were not unique in believing, "The more frightening the prospect of a summer in Mississippi, the more obliged we felt to be there." Still, it was difficult for most volunteers to believe they might die or be seriously hurt. "I discovered, however, that no one was weighing risk against need in *personal* terms," volunteer Stephen Bingham recalled. "When discussing the realism of death in Mississippi, one did not speak about his own death but about someone else's." Even after Schwerner, Chaney, and Goodman were reported missing, the volunteers' first instincts were to downplay the seriousness of the news. As Sally Belfrage wrote, "To think of it in other terms was to be forced to identify with the three, to be prepared, irrevocably, to give one's life."[15]

But as the weight of what had probably happened to the three began to sink in, it became much easier for volunteers to admit, as one wrote, "I am scared shitless." Nancy Jervis recalled overhearing a phone conversation in which Andrew Goodman reassured his mother, "Don't worry, I'm going to a CORE area. It's safer." For most volunteers, just watching the evening news was enough to make them realize that Andrew Goodman's fate could be theirs. "I cannot begin to tell you how it feels to be here," a Freedom School teacher wrote home. "They were in Oxford only a few days before—they couldn't already be in such danger. But then all of a sudden—the disbelief is countered by a vivid picture of reality—that it could be you." In a searing letter written on her fourth day at Oxford, Margaret Aley acknowledged, "The reality of Mississippi gets closer to us every day. We know the blood is going to flow this summer, and it's going to be our blood. And I'm scared—I'm very scared."[16]

After the first orientation session, the volunteers left Ohio with a sense that if what lay ahead was to be feared, it was also a great adventure. "Kids were hanging out the windows kissing and hugging friends from the moving bus. It was a strange conglomeration of children headed for summer camp and children going off to war," Ellen Lake remembered. "Finally the buses gathered speed and left us behind. Wordlessly, as if pulled by some strong magnet, we silently formed a circle and, joining hands, sang, 'We'll Never Turn

Back' very slowly and solemnly. Afterwards, we broke up silently and moved apart. Overhead, the omen had changed: the sun came bursting through the clouds."[17]

By the second orientation session, the day of departure was grim. "As we were preparing to leave at the end of a serious week of training, it seemed as though we were going into a foreign country or a police state," Sandra Hard observed. In her description of the last meeting of staff and volunteers, Pam Parker recalled, "The group sang in one voice, each individual singing not for himself but for the group. Tears ran down many faces, brought forth for the future sufferings of others going to Mississippi and for those already there who will suffer the consequences of our coming."[18]

At last the Summer Project was on the kind of wartime footing its organizers had been seeking. It was no longer possible to say of the volunteers, as Cleveland Sellers once had, "Many of them talked about Mississippi as if it were somehow the same as the romanticized scenes they had read about in *Gone with the Wind*." The romance of the Summer Project was over, as was the idea that a white college student might be safer than a black SNCC field secretary. No one on the way to Mississippi could doubt the dangers that lay ahead or the likelihood, as Bob Moses warned, "There may be more deaths."[19]

7

The Magnolia Jungle

July was officially scheduled to be "Hospitality Month" in Mississippi, but in late June, as the volunteers and staff of the Summer Project began settling into the Mississippi countryside, the world they found, as one volunteer put it, was a "magnolia jungle." Earlier in the year, in a letter to SNCC supporters, Bob Moses had felt compelled to deny the charge that SNCC was "launching this project to incite violence and chaos in Mississippi." Now, in a letter to the parents of the Summer Project volunteers, he again pledged restraint. "We are," he promised, "specifically avoiding any demonstrations for integrated facilities, as we do not feel the state is ready to permit such activity at this time. All workers, staff and Summer Volunteers alike, are pledged to nonviolence in all situations."[1]

But Moses knew that such caution would not be enough to protect the volunteers. More help was needed from the federal government. In the same letter in which he tried to reassure the parents of the volunteers, he urged them to use whatever power they had to spur the FBI and the Justice Department to action. "We are asking all parents to use their influence in the coming week to pressure President Johnson and Attorney General Kennedy into a commitment to protect workers *before* violence occurs, instead of waiting until the worst has happened before they offer their help," Moses wrote. "Unless the President and the Attorney General can be convinced of the need for federal protection of civil rights workers in Mississippi, the events of Philadelphia are almost certain to be repeated over and over again in the next two months."[2]

"We hope you are making preparations to have bond money available in the event of your arrest," the volunteers were told in the first memo they received from the Mississippi Summer Project committee. The new reality of the volunteers' lives was epitomized by the Security Handbook they were given before leaving Oxford, Ohio. Like the Boy Scout Handbook, the Summer Project Security Handbook was filled with practical advice. It left little to chance. "Know all roads in and out of town. Study the county map. Know locations of sanctuaries and safe homes in the county," the handbook advised. "When getting out of a car at night, make sure the car's inside light is out. Be conscious of cars which circle offices or Freedom Houses. Take license numbers of all suspicious cars." Impossible to ignore, however, was that this practical advice was designed to prevent its reader from being murdered. The "don'ts" of the Security Handbook made that point unmistakable. "If it can be avoided, try not to sleep near open windows. Do not stand in doorways at night with the light at your back. At night people should not sit in their rooms without drawn shades. Do not congregate in front of the house at night." Even the handbook's dress code was preoccupied with murder. A volunteer did not have to be a subtle reader to see that authors of the handbook had camouflage, not decorum, in mind when they warned, "Try to avoid bizarre or provocative clothing, and beards."[3]

Unlike Bob Moses's letter to parents, the Security Handbook was not written for public consumption. The advice it offered reflected the organizers' deepest fears about the coming months. The disappearance of Michael Schwerner, James Chaney, and Andrew Goodman twenty-four hours after their arrival in Mississippi from Ohio more than justified those fears, but the advice the handbook offered made sense in any case. For the Summer Project volunteers, the war in Mississippi—in contrast to the one in Vietnam—would be their 1960s good war, but as members of a nonviolent army prepared to be killed but not to kill, they were uniquely vulnerable. In anticipation of their coming, Mississippi had been whipped into a state of invasion frenzy that made it open season on anyone associated with the Summer Project.

"A Major Purpose of Invaders Is to Attract Federal Occupation," the *Jackson Clarion-Ledger* warned in the headline of its lead editorial for June 30, and in its news section scarcely a day went by when the *Clarion-Ledger* failed to carry a major story on the "race agitation groups" behind the Summer Project. Other Mississippi papers were equally sensationalistic. "Mississippians Not Going to Be Run Over," the *Columbus Commercial Dispatch* declared. "Students Go Home," urged a headline in the *Natchez Democrat*. It was yellow journalism at its worst, but Mississippi's newspapers were doing little more than taking a cue from the state's leading politicians. "If we allow these invaders to succeed in their dastardly scheme," Governor Paul Johnson warned, "we will be guilty of a very costly error."[4]

Governor Johnson and the state legislature had wasted no time in putting Mississippi on a wartime footing as soon as they learned of plans for the Summer Project. The state highway patrol was expanded from 275 to 475 men and given police power to quell civil disorders and conduct undercover investigations. At the same time laws were passed to criminalize the kinds of civil rights activities that the Summer Project organizers were thought to be planning. By the start of June the state had passed bills outlawing the picketing of public buildings and the distribution of leaflets calling for economic boycotts. Under Mississippi law it was now possible for an arrested civil rights worker to be transferred to Parchman State Prison from a local jail, and for the police of one city to be shared by another during "riots and civil disturbances."[5]

Local officials soon followed the state's lead. In Jackson, the state capital, Mayor Allen Thompson turned his city into an armed camp. A year earlier NAACP leader Medgar Evers had described Jackson as "a city of over 150,000, of which 40 percent is Negro, in which there is not a single Negro policeman or policewoman, school crossing guard, fireman, clerk, stenographer or supervisor employed in any city department or the mayor's office in other than menial capacities, except those employed in segregated facilities." In the summer of 1964 Mayor Thompson's answer to such criticism and the threat of racial protest was to build his police force from 390 to 450 and, with a $2.2 million budget, buy two hundred new shotguns, stockpile tear gas, and issue gas masks to every man in his force. The pride of the mayor's police force quickly became a thirteen-thousand-pound armored personnel carrier, nicknamed the Thompson Tank, which was outfitted with twelve-gauge steel walls and bulletproof windows.[6]

It mattered little that the rioting to be put down by the Thompson Tank never materialized, or that the detention compounds built by the mayor to hold twenty-five thousand prisoners were never used. A white Mississippi politician was in trouble only if he did not take the Summer Project seriously. In the context of invasion frenzy, the volunteers could be held responsible for anything that went wrong. "If violence erupts," Mississippi Senator John Stennis declared, "the blood will be on the hands of those who formed and led this invasion into a state where they were not welcome or invited." Stennis's sentiments were echoed by Mayor Jim Burt of McComb. "I don't care what the devil happens to these people who come in here to stir up trouble," Burt warned. "If the monkey is on anyone's back, it is not on ours—it's on the people who come down here."[7]

The meaning of such disclaimers to those who would do violence in the coming months was clear: they had a green light to do as they pleased. In July the Ku Klux Klan's official Mississippi publication, the *Klan Ledger*, announced, "We are not going to sit back and permit our rights and the rights of our posterity to be negotiated away by a group composed of atheistic priests, brain-washed black savages, and mongrelized money-worshippers, meeting with some stupid or cowardly politician. Take heed, atheists and mongrels, we will not travel your path to Leninist Hall, but we will buy YOU a ticket to the Eternal if you insist." The threat from the National States' Rights party was equally explicit. "You are right about one thing—this is going to be a long hot summer—but the 'heat' will be applied to the race mixing TRASH by the DECENT people," a letter to SNCC warned. "When your communist-oriented goons get to Mississippi, I hope they get their just dues." None of these threats could be taken lightly. As the summer approached, the Klan began holding open rallies, and new organizations like the Association for the Preservation of the White Race expanded so rapidly that they ceased being marginal.[8]

A week after J. Edgar Hoover's July 10 opening of the FBI's new Jackson office, seven black churches were burned to the ground in Mississippi, and in an editorial entitled "God Help the USA" the *Meridian Star* summed up the resentment that most white Mississippians would feel all summer long toward the White House and the Summer Project. "We do not blame Mr. Hoover in the least. He is a dedicated public servant. We believe he was sent to Mississippi by President Lyndon Johnson who cannot do enough to prove to COFO that he is their devoted slave," the *Star* editorial charged. The *Star* warned its readers to prepare themselves for an ordeal in which "the student volunteers— the beatniks, the wild-eyed left wing nuts, the unshaven and unwashed trash and the just plain stupid or ignorant or misled—go on meddling with things about which they know nothing and which concern them not."[9]

As they began the long drive to Mississippi, it was easy for the volunteers to sentimentalize the orientation they had just completed. However difficult their conflicts with the Summer Project staff, they had been shared conflicts in "a place where no one disapproved of what you were doing." In Mississippi the volunteers would still be a part of a collective drama, but now they would be an isolated minority. As volunteer Gene Nelson observed, "You're so isolated here that you can easily forget about the rest of the world. You can even forget about the rest of the country you're working in."[10]

In Ohio a volunteer had written to his family, "It is impossible for you to imagine what we are going into, as it is for me now." As they poured into Mississippi, doubts resurfaced among the volunteers. "My mind still stumbles on the realization that I'm actually going to Mississippi," Jan Handke wrote. "Like Bosco being poured into milk, much of my experience is still sitting on the surface of my mind. It hasn't sunk down, much less been assimilated into my other nineteen years of experience." To the volunteers, Mississippi was, as one put it, "enemy territory." Crossing into the state frightened them. "I awoke with fear gripping my gut. I had a hard time forcing down breakfast," a volunteer on his way to Ruleville wrote of the morning he crossed into Mississippi. A volunteer getting off the bus in Moss Point assumed she was going to be arrested when she was met by the local sheriff. "I was scared silly at first, and was already fumbling in my pocket to make sure I had a dime for my one call from jail," she recalled.[11]

The volunteers' first task was to adjust to their fears, to hone them into survival skills which would protect them. It was not easy. Margaret Aley found herself in danger before she ever got off the bus to Greenwood. "When we were about a mile outside of Greenwood, a police car followed us into town, and there were four police cars at the bus depot when we arrived," she reported in her first letter home from Mississippi. "The police followed, and all day they kept circling the office, as a buzzard would circle a dead animal." Phil Moore quickly learned that having a telephone could be a liability. "I wake up in the morning sighing with relief that I was not bombed," he wrote. "Even as I write this letter, we are told that our office might be bombed by an anonymous voice."[12]

The volunteers who were of most use to the Summer Project were those who realized their whole way of life had to be changed. As Clark Gardener, a volunteer staying in Carthage, observed, "Someone said at Oxford at the orientation session that once you are in Mississippi, everything outside it seems unreal—there is a lot of truth in it." It was particularly necessary for the volunteers to understand that although they brought the concern of the media and the federal government with them neither reporters nor Justice Department officials would do them much good on an isolated country road. Middle-class assumptions about the workings of the law had to be set aside. "You grow up in a safe middle-class scene, and then you're a pariah. All the instruments of the law and the institutions of law are your enemy," volunteer Marshall Ganz recalled. "There is a whole sort of reversal, which for someone of my background was an utterly new experience, and a lonely one and a frightening one." Volunteer Robbie Osman, who was badly beaten in Jackson, used similar language to describe the sense of vulnerability he felt after his beating. "We take so much for granted that we don't believe can be violated. When somebody sails through that protection and does violence to your body, the next time you walk down the street, you're no longer surrounded by the illusion of safety," he remembered.[13]

In a state that looked on their coming as an invasion, the volunteers' day-to-day survival depended on the ability of the black communities in which they lived to provide them with a haven. "I hardly saw white people. I felt safe in the black community," Nancy Jervis recalled of her time in Madison County. And from Greenville, Nancy Schieffelin wrote to her parents, "We eat in Negro restaurants, frequent only Negro joints. The Negroes are our security. The white man in the car is a threat."[14]

Knowing the rules and following them were, however, two different matters. The volunteers' early letters home are filled with complaints about the routines they must follow. "We can go nowhere alone or at night," a volunteer isolated in the countryside quickly realized. "All doors must be locked. All shades drawn. The overhead light in the car must be disconnected." Nothing could be done by instinct. "I remember putting blankets over the windows if we were doing something at night," Lewis Hyde recalled. "It was an odd combination of being generally afraid all the time, yet most of the time nothing that bad happened." Hardest of all was the feeling of being constantly on guard. "The enemy is hidden, and there are no obvious times for him to become visible. At any time, in the street, in a shop, or driving on the road, someone may start something," Ron de Sousa wrote in his notebooks. Even in Greenwood, where SNCC had its summer headquarters and a large staff, there was always tension. "It is the fear and uncertainty that is maddening. I must always be on guard," a Greenwood volunteer wrote. "I do not know what to expect but always know to expect something."[15]

As the summer progressed, this tension took its toll. Dennis Flannigan lost thirty pounds and by the time he left Mississippi weighed just 135. For others the price was psychological. "Violence hangs overhead like dead air—it hangs here and maybe it'll fall and maybe it won't," a Ruleville volunteer complained. In Holly Springs, voter registration worker Peter Cummings found, "The constant harassment, the knowledge of danger breeds a tension that even jokes and laughter never throw off." Nonetheless, by midsummer most volunteers found a way to cope with the dangers they faced. As Linda Davis, currently chief of the criminal section of the Civil Rights Division of the Justice Department, recalled, "The first few nights we twitched at every noise, but you can only live in fear so long." The volunteers learned, as Sally Belfrage put it, "to live with fear as a condition, like heat or night." Like the project staff, the volunteers now worried about anybody who did *not* show fear. As one volunteer wrote to her brother, "Anyone who comes down here and is not afraid I think must be crazy as well as dangerous to this project where security is quite important."[16]

Even jail, the volunteers found, could be endured. The

trauma of being behind bars for the first time in their lives left most volunteers angry and exhausted, but it also returned them to the project with a greater sense of confidence. Another threat ceased being a threat. In Hattiesburg Ron Ridenour and Howard Kirchenbaum discovered that after their initial fears they were able to cope with being placed in cells in which black, then white, prisoners were encouraged by the police to beat them up. In the Greenwood jail Margaret Aley became so weak after a hunger strike that she blacked out twice; but on her release from jail she had no trouble returning to work or turning her experience into a story, "Abuse in Dixie Jail," published in the *San Francisco Chronicle*. Aley and her fellow workers even had the satisfaction of leaving their own "memorials" in the Greenwood jail, carefully writing "We Shall Overcome" on their cell wall and drawing a picture of two clasped hands, one black and one white.[17]

The volunteers' most important adjustment, however, was not in learning to cope with white Mississippi but in learning to be at home in black Mississippi. Most of the volunteers' time was spent among blacks, and it was their trust the volunteers needed for the Summer Project to be successful. The difficulty was that few of the volunteers came from social backgrounds in which contact with blacks was an everyday occurrence. In the case of well-to-do volunteers, the blacks they most often knew were, as one put it, "the people who have always appeared to me as servants."[18]

A Canton volunteer who observed, "We weren't quite ready for what we found," spoke for the majority of volunteers. Their initial reaction to the poverty of black Mississippi was shock. "The wood and tarpaper shacks were unpainted, erupting from the centers of fields, their outhouses leaning grotesquely askew nearby," Sally Belfrage observed as she entered Mississippi for the first time. "The houses simply sagged as though about to melt into the ground. Shimmering in the heat mirage, they looked utterly insubstantial and invented." Up close the volunteers saw that what they had glimpsed from their cars was no illusion. "In my whole life I have never seen poverty on such a massive scale," Margaret Aley wrote. "If the house I'm staying in were in a California suburban residential district, it would have been condemned and burned long ago."[19]

"The poverty and sorrow of the neighborhoods doesn't leave you. I've been to hundreds of houses I could kick down with my feet and a small hammer," a Meridian volunteer wrote. In Itta Bena a stunned volunteer found that time did not diminish his first impression of the poverty around him. "To see the place in the real is so different from seeing pictures of it," he wrote. "You feel the heat, breathe the dust, smell the outhouses, hear the kids and the chickens." Time did, however, make the volunteers increasingly aware of the human dimensions of the poverty around them. "I saw other children today who bore the marks of the Negro in rural Mississippi. One had a protruding navel the size of the stone he held in his hand. Several had distended stomachs. Is America really the land that greets its visitors with 'Send me your tired, your poor, your helpless masses to breathe free'?" a Shaw volunteer wrote. Heather Tobis remembered thinking, "Here we are in America. I can be in a place where there are dirt roads and no indoor plumbing and kids get worms through their feet because they don't have shoes."[20]

As they took up residence in black homes and neighborhoods, the volunteers quickly became more than observers of life in black Mississippi. They became part of it. They learned to overcome their embarrassment at using a chamber pot, found that an old-fashioned wringer washer worked just fine, and discovered that even without indoor plumbing a bath was possible. "There were three of us in one bed, so I learned to sleep without moving," Greenville volunteer Pat Vail remembered. "I took a bath. But no ordinary bath," a Mileston volunteer proudly wrote home. "We take this bucket out in the back yard and fill it with water warmed over a fire. It's pitch black so we shine Mr. Clark's lights on the bucket. Then I strip down naked and stand in the bucket wash. That is the way you take a bath around here."[21]

The volunteers also faced problems that no amount of ingenuity could overcome. "There are people here without food and clothing. Kids that eat a bit of bread for breakfast, chicken necks for dinner. Kids that don't have clothes to go to school in," a Ruleville volunteer learned. And in Shaw a volunteer sadly noted, "The other America is opening itself before my naive, middle-class eyes. The cockroaches draw patterns across the floor and table and make a live patchwork on the bed. Sweat covers my skin and cakes brown in my joints—wrist, elbow, knee, neck." As the summer wore on, what changed most in the volunteers was their understanding of "how much it took to be a Negro in Mississippi twelve months a year for a lifetime." The July 4 letter of a Hattiesburg volunteer begins, "Every time I talk to people, I hear about things which bring tears to my eyes." Then suddenly the tone of the letter changes, and what emerges is the volunteer's identification with the people he has earlier been observing. "I have begun, finally, to feel deep inside me the horrible double existence Negroes have to lead, the strategies they must learn to survive without going crazy or being physically maimed—or destroyed." Now the volunteers understood why even an event as politically important as the president's signing of the Civil Rights Act seemed remote to anyone black and living in rural Mississippi. "Watching the signing was a moment of happiness and a pain of hurt," a Clarksdale volunteer wrote. "People here in Clarksdale all know about that bill but tomorrow and Saturday, the 4th of July, they will still be in the cotton fields making three dollars a day. They'll still be in white homes working as maids, making three dollars a day."[22]

• • •

The physical courage of the families sheltering them was immediately apparent to the volunteers. Here were people who had gotten along for years by blending into the countryside, and now they were giving up all that protection. "If they throw a bomb we'll die with you," Christopher Wilson was told by the family with whom he stayed. It was a frightening thought to Wilson, but as he and the other volunteers knew, they only had to survive the summer. The families sheltering them had signed up for a war without a foreseeable end.[23]

There were so many ways these families could be hurt. Few had savings they could fall back on in a crisis. Many depended on breadwinners whose jobs could be terminated at the whim of a white employer. Even self-sufficient black farmers were taking a big financial risk in housing a volunteer. As Holly Springs voter registration worker Robert Feinglass discovered from his canvassing, "Nearly everyone in black Mississippi is at least a year in debt. The threat of suspended credit and foreclosures is a tremendous burden; our presence adds much to that load."[24]

After their Ohio orientation the volunteers were prepared to have their motives doubted by the families who sheltered them. They assumed that the feelings of SNCC veterans were similar to those they would encounter in Mississippi, but this did not prove to be so. Time and again the volunteers were received with a warmth they found overwhelming. "The people have been wonderful. The welcome has been so wonderful that I've been at loose ends figuring out ways of being worth it," Gene Nelson wrote from Holmes County. And in Gulfport Ellen Lake had the same reaction to her reception: "It's amazing how hospitable people are: everywhere we go—to bars and restaurants—we're told that the bill has been paid for us," she wrote to her parents. "Last night the three girls on the project were invited by a local woman for dinner, which was delicious."[25]

Under these circumstances it was essential for the volunteers to be careful that the kindness they received did not become the deference toward whites which they were struggling to overcome. It was a sensitive task, and those who succeeded at it did so by trusting their instincts. A young medical student in Meridian learned when not to be professional. "I gave medical advice this week to a father whose son had an abscess on his chest," he reported. "The father thanked me and kissed my hand. I was embarrassed and didn't know what to do, so I kissed his hand." Sally Belfrage, staying with the Amos family in Greenwood, had to use her authority in order to deny it. Unable to persuade Mr. Amos to sit down while she was eating, Belfrage realized "in some extraordinary paradox he would not think of us as equals until I ordered him to. I begged him to sit down; he wouldn't. I *told* him to sit down. He did, in great confusion. Somehow or another, everything was all right after that."[26]

Such barriers were not always possible to cross. The volunteers often found themselves on display at the houses in which they stayed. Frequently the neighbors would file in to have a look, and among the children there was a special fascination. Even with the best of intentions, some feelings were too ingrained to be changed over a summer. "Sometimes you feel you're getting there when a woman tells you about her fears and tells how she lies to the white folks but secretly hates them," Geoff Cowan wrote. "But a white man never turns black in Mississippi. There are still the long silences and the incomprehensible phrases. Women still call you Mr. Geoff instead of Geoff, and old men offer their chairs. That doesn't disappear when they start to talk about fear."[27]

Nonetheless, breakthroughs were possible for the volunteers who kept at it. By mid-summer many of them and the families they were staying with had grown close. Often the closeness could be described only in self-conscious terms. "I have become so close to the family I am staying with—eleven people—that Mrs. H. finally paid me a great compliment," a Holmes County volunteer wrote to her mother. "She was introducing me to one of her Negro women friends and said, 'This is Nancy, my adopted daughter.' " But there was also a closeness that could be natural and showed up in daily routines. "People bring over a dozen eggs or a cake or invite us to dinner. The hospitality seems like that of the old frontier, with its house raisings and quilting bees," a Gulfport volunteer noted. The neighbors of the family with whom Irene Paull was staying were astonished to find her sweeping the floor and washing the dishes after dinner, but much to Paull's relief, the woman who had taken her in found no need to defend what Paull was doing. "Can't you see, I've gone and got myself a white girl," the neighbors were laughingly told.[28]

Those volunteers who experienced such breakthroughs invariably came away believing that Mississippi had done much more for them than they had done for Mississippi. As Margaret Aley later observed, "Just because I left Mississippi, Mississippi did not leave me." But it was not only the volunteers and the black families sheltering them who were affected by these small triumphs. So was the credibility of the Summer Project. The everyday victories gave a reality to the political hope that Bob Moses had voiced in June when he told the volunteers, "If we can go and come back alive, then that is something. If you can go into Negro homes and just sit and talk, that will be a huge job."[29]

8

Pinto Beans
and Politics

Throughout the summer of 1964 the volunteers were continually reminded that the bonds they were establishing within the black community were changing Mississippi politically. "I remember cooking some pinto beans—that's all we had—and everybody just got around the pot, you know, and that was an experience just to see white people coming around the pot and getting a bowl," Unita Blackwell, who later in the summer would become a delegate of the new Freedom Democratic party, recalled. "People began to feel that they wasn't just helpless anymore, that they had come together."[1] It was nonetheless essential, the volunteers realized, to push on with the specific tasks they had been assigned in their guerrilla war—establishing Freedom Schools, carrying out voter registration, and helping to build a Mississippi Freedom Democratic party which would challenge the all-white Mississippi Democrats.

For the volunteers the question was how to pursue these tasks, especially in areas that just a year earlier Bob Moses had described to a House Judiciary Committee as "too dangerous for whites." The volunteers quickly discovered that most of what they needed to know came to them by trial and error. Their past experience, particularly what they had learned in college, was more of a liability than a help.[2]
1960s were over would prove instrumental in persuading the government to begin Head Start, the volunteers began with a framework that SNCC had decided upon in late 1963. The idea for the schools originated with Charlie Cobb, now a staff writer for the *National Geographic*. Cobb had dropped out of Howard University to come to Mississippi in 1962. His experience there convinced him that any Summer Project designed to change Mississippi must include a school program to deal with the problems faced by black children.

As one of only two states in the nation without a mandatory education law, Mississippi provided young blacks with few incentives to stay in school. In 1960 the median years of school completed by all blacks over the age of twenty-five was just six. Forty-two percent of all whites had managed to finish high school, but only 7 percent of the black population had done so. In rural areas black schools were routinely closed for weeks during the fall so that their pupils could pick cotton, and on average the state schools spent nearly four times as much for white children ($81.86) as for black children ($21.77). What most angered Cobb was that even within Mississippi's black schools the values of white

Mississippi were taught. In some areas school superinten-
dents even forbade teaching black students the history of Reconstruction. "The State of Mississippi destroys 'smart niggers'
and its classrooms remain intellectual wastelands," Cobb
wrote. "There are Negro students who have been thrown out of
classes for asking questions about the freedom rides or voting.
Negro teachers have been fired for saying the wrong thing."[3]

The Freedom School program originally proposed by
Cobb was modest in scale. He suggested running Freedom
Schools during July and August and offering instruction to
tenth- and eleventh-grade students, who would then return to
their regular classes in the fall. The Freedom School students
would receive tutoring in subjects they were already taking,
but the thrust of the Freedom School program, like that of the
Summer Project, would be political. "The overall theme of
the school would be the student as a force for social change
in Mississippi," Cobb explained. "If we are concerned with
breaking the power structure, then we have to be concerned
with building up our own institutions to replace the old,
unjust, decadent ones which make up the existing power
structure. Education in Mississippi is an institution which can
be validly replaced."[4]

With four or five students to a single teacher, Cobb was
convinced his program had a good chance of succeeding, and
in memos to SNCC's executive committee he stressed the
practicality of his proposal. "The Freedom School should
have a special appeal for many of the students planning to
come to Mississippi this summer, as it would be a project
they could follow through from the beginning to the end—
watch develop—and would have some definition," he wrote.
"As the summer program for Mississippi now shapes up, it
seems as if hundreds of students as well as professional
educators from some of the best universities and colleges in
the North will be coming to Mississippi to lend themselves to
the movement. These are some of the best minds in the

country, and their academic value ought to be recognized and used to advantage." As it turned out, Cobb needed no hard sell. His proposals elicited widespread approval within SNCC, and by spring plans were completed for a series of Freedom Schools throughout Mississippi. Their curriculum would be based on case studies drawn on the students' own experiences with racism, supplemented by a curriculum guide focused on black history. Heading the schools would be Yale professor Staughton Lynd, a political activist and the former chairman of the history department at Spelman College in Atlanta.[5]

It was a good plan, but in a Freedom School project that never had enough books to go around or more than two thousand dollars to spend over the entire summer, a curriculum guide and director could do little more than suggest how classes might be run. "I was an itinerant bureaucrat," Lynd later confessed. "I saw a play in Holly Springs, an adult class in Indianola, a preschool mass meeting in McComb." Lynd was being modest, but he was also indicating how impossible it was to supervise the Freedom Schools. As they struggled to get their individual schools going, the volunteers were essentially on their own. "You'll meet on someone's lawn under a tree. You'll tear up the curriculum and teach what you know," a SNCC staffer told the volunteers during orientation. It was the best advice they would get. The more they forgot about what school had been like for them, the more effective they would be as teachers.[6]

To begin with, it was necessary for the volunteers to change their ideas of what a school should look like. "We are one of the few Freedom Schools with a building of its own and classrooms and desks and blackboards," a Meridian volunteer wrote to her parents. She was not exaggerating her good fortune. Schwerner, Chaney, and Goodman had disappeared following a visit to a church which had been fire-bombed after its congregation gave permission for its use as a Freedom School; throughout the summer, intimidation and a

shortage of usable buildings made Freedom School accom-
modations hard to come by. "We gathered on benches under
the trees," was a familiar first-day comment. The successful
Freedom School teacher quickly realized that the school was
a state of mind beyond all else. "I'm sitting in what we've
turned into a Freedom School—a one-room wooden church,"
a proud Canton volunteer wrote. "Most of the windows are
half-paneless. The only seats resemble benches." In Har-
mony, getting the Freedom School ready became a community effort. "About 20 adults, teens, and young kids began to
come to help clean out this gigantic school house, abandoned
for over 6 years," an ecstatic volunteer reported. "It was a
miracle—just like *Lilies of the Field*. We sorted good and
usable books from others, knocked all the loose glass out of
the windows, 3 & 4 year olds were sweeping out rooms and
carrying books to a huge fire where we were burning all the
trash. In less than two hours, we were even pouring water
over the floors and scrubbing them clean."[7]

The volunteers also had to adjust to teaching a student
body of all ages. Once a community gave its support to a
Freedom School, it became a gathering place for anyone who
wanted to learn. In Greenville, Nancy Schieffelin found,
"Little kids from the ages of four to ten have been coming in
swarms. The Freedom Schools aren't really here to serve the
younger set, but we couldn't turn them away." Nor was it
possible to turn away parents of Freedom School students
when they too decided they wanted to learn to read. The
most successful Freedom Schools were those that met whatever needs a community had—whether for adult education or
day care. To accommodate twenty adults, most of whom
were farmers, the Freedom School in Benton County moved a
class from the morning to six o'clock in the evening. In Ruleville schedules were changed so that the school could have a
nursery in the morning. The task of caring for the children,
some as young as five months, proved more difficult than ex-

pected, but as volunteer Kirsty Powell noted, the nursery "was important not just because it made the attendance of the mothers possible, but for its own sake." The nursery showed that in Ruleville the needs of those using the school, not the convenience of those running it, would dictate decisions.[8]

The biggest adjustment the Freedom School teachers had to make was, however, in how they taught. Most of them had been educated in conventional, middle-class school systems. What had worked for them in suburbia was often not what worked best in Mississippi. "Because of the peculiar nature of a Freedom School, formal teaching methods must be modified," a Holly Springs teacher found. In Hattiesburg it was the same story. "Much of what we know about teaching must be unlearned or relearned here. The standard academic approach has not worked at all well," teachers there discovered. In a conventional school system such a diagnosis would have put teacher and student in conflict. But in Mississippi it led the volunteers to realize that if their students were given an active role in class, energies were released that had been bottled up by years of Mississippi schooling. A Holly Springs volunteer wrote: "They are a sharp group. But they are under-educated and starved for knowledge. They know that they have been cheated, and they want anything and everything that we can give them." In Meridian another Freedom School teacher observed, "One thing that I've found here is that the students are on a much higher level than I had been led to expect. A lot of books which I wouldn't think of bringing because they would be 'on too high a level' or 'too intellectual' are being used very successfully. If reading levels are not always the highest, the philosophical understanding is almost alarming: some of the things that our eleven and twelve years olds will come out with would never be expected from someone of that age in the North."[9]

As the volunteers became more attuned to their students, the form of their classes changed. Students were given more freedom to role-play. They were helped to start school newspapers. They were offered workshops in voter registration and picketing. They were encouraged to call their teachers by their first names. It did not take the students and their parents long to realize the importance of what was happening. In one Freedom School after another, overcrowding became the great problem, and in towns like McComb, going to Freedom School became the students' way of showing where they stood politically. The day after the McComb Freedom School was firebombed, seventy-five children showed up for their next morning's class.[10]

Still, the growth of the Freedom Schools left some teachers dissatisfied. In Shaw a frustrated volunteer wrote Staughton Lynd, "Running a freedom school is an absurd waste of time. I don't want to sit around in a classroom; I want to go out and throw a few bombs, burn a few office buildings, not to injure people but to shake them up." But for most volunteers the Freedom School experience was a good one. They left Mississippi convinced that they had made a difference. An Indianola volunteer wrote, "I can see the change. The 16 year old's discovery of poetry, of Whitman and Cummings and above all the struggle to express thoughts in words, to translate ideas into concrete written words. After two weeks a child finally looks me in the eye, unafraid, acknowledging a bond of trust which 300 years of Mississippians said should never, could never exist. I can feel the growth of self-confidence." In Holly Springs Pam Parker used similar language to describe her students. "The atmosphere in class is unbelievable. It is what every teacher dreams about—real, honest enthusiasm and desire to learn anything and everything," Parker wrote to her parents. "They drain me of everything that I have to offer so that I go home at night completely exhausted."[11]

The teachers who were most sensitive to what was happening in the Freedom Schools worried not whether their students were equal to them but whether they were equal to their students. Despite the success of her classes, Pam Parker acknowledged, "I feel inadequate to the task of teaching them, but I keep saying to myself that as long as I continue to feel humble there is a chance that we might all learn a whole lot together." Even the professional teachers in the Freedom Schools were not immune from such fears. "At home some students start off the year with a 'show me' attitude. Here they have a blind faith that you have something to offer them," Karol Nelson, a California teacher in Madison County, observed. "Working with them sometimes makes me ashamed for myself, because I'm not always sure I can live up to their faith."[12]

The Freedom Schools concluded with a student convention on August 8 and 9 in Meridian. There the student delegates worked out a platform with resolutions on everything from the new Civil Rights Act to the government's responsibility for ending job discrimination. For the student delegates, the convention offered a chance to see what had been happening in Freedom Schools across the state as well as a sense of closure. But the convention was also important for the teachers. Before the summer began, organizers had worried about the Freedom Schools. Many had wondered if in the Mississippi heat they would draw enough students to make an impact. Director Staughton Lynd had been nervous about the contrast between the "predominantly white" Freedom School teachers and the "almost-all-Negro" SNCC voter registration staff. The estimated three thousand students who attended Freedom Schools over the course of the summer answered the first concern, and the resolutions passed by the student delegates at their convention answered the second. It was not only possible for the volunteers to see they had made an impact on the students, it was also possible to believe, as departing Freedom School teacher Alvin Pam wrote, "The children we reached will certainly 'infect' others with their new-found curiosity and daring."[13]

For those volunteers doing voter registration work, success was much harder to come by. Within the Summer Project, voter registration was considered the most important work. As Bob Moses observed in June, "We think the key is the vote. Any change, any possibility for dissidence and opposition, depends first on a political breakthrough." But what made voter registration so important was also what made it so difficult and dangerous. The idea of a Freedom School or of blacks and whites living together was anathema to white Mississippi. "Must have fast car" was part of the job description for teaching in Issaquena and Sharkey counties. But what went on in a Freedom School or a private house in the black section of town could also be ignored. Neither directly intruded on the white community; neither promised an immediate change in the balance of political power. Voter registration, on the other hand, was a threat that whites could not ignore. In 1962 there were five counties in Mississippi with a majority black population and not a single registered black voter. In those counties, or in any county where the black and white populations were nearly equal, everything from the election of sheriffs to the paving of streets would be subject to change if blacks suddenly won political power that reflected their numbers.[14]

As they began canvassing for blacks who were willing to go to the courthouse and try to register, the volunteers found themselves in a difficult position. In contrast to the Freedom School teacher who came with a skill to give, the voter registration worker came with a demand to make. To refuse that demand was to own up to being afraid, but to do as the voter registration worker asked was to take a terrible chance with little likelihood of actually making it onto the voter rolls. Mississippi law gave county registrars the right to decide if voters were qualified by making them pass a test that, among other things, required them to interpret any of 286 sections of the Mississippi constitution. The test was subjective, and an applicant could be failed for any reason a registrar thought appropriate.[15]

As a consequence, most applicants did fail. As voter registration worker Charles Stewart noted in a report on the Summer Project which he wrote in September, "We certainly did not make any gigantic breakthroughs in registration." The statistics show that by the end of the summer, seventeen thousand blacks had filled out Mississippi voter registration forms, but of these fewer than seventeen hundred made it onto the voter registration rolls—and most of these (nine hundred) came from Panola County, where federal officials oversaw voting procedures after a successful presummer lawsuit.[16]

It did not take the voter registration workers many visits to black homes to realize just where they stood. Time and again they found that in this role their whiteness was a much greater liability than they had foreseen. "You meet an afraid, but sometimes, eager, curious face—one which is used to many times over seventy years' worth of saying 'Yes Sir' to everything a white man says—and not really listening," a Clarksdale volunteer wrote. In Holly Springs Robert Feinglass found that his color tended to strain any first visit to a black family. "When we walk up to a house, there are always children out front. They look up and see white men in a car, and fear and caution cover their expression," Feinglass wrote. "The children run up to their parents, hide behind them. We walk up, smile, say howdy, and hold out our hands. As we shake hands, I tell them my name. They tell me their names, and I say Mr. _____, how do you do. It is likely the first time in the life of this farmer or housewife a white man has ever shaken hands with them, or even called them with a handle to their names. This does not bode well to them; they are suspicious." Even if he won the cooperation of the families he was trying to help register, Feinglass realized, some doubts would not disappear. "We talk about dignity. People listen and wonder. They are not sure. What does it mean when a white man tells them the truth, when he asks them to help him, to help themselves? Why is he here? What does he really want? What will come of it?"[17]

Such doubts were only the first hurdle faced by voter registration workers. White retaliation was the most difficult problem for Summer Project workers and local blacks alike. Often local whites did not even wait for a voter registration worker to complete his rounds before they began making threats. "Last evening we went up to Drew, the tough little town north of here to do some canvassing. Whites streamed through the area. Sometimes they would call a Negro over to their car and send him scampering back to his house. The police kept talking into their mikes as they cruised by," a Ruleville volunteer reported. "We talked about the whole movement and about how you were safer if the community was united. This evening we will go back again and talk to the people a bit, just to show them we are still around."[18]

But as everyone knew, the volunteers could not always be around to help. The names of those who applied to vote were published in local papers for two weeks, and every black family had a story about what had happened to them or to a neighbor who tried to register. "Negroes talk freely about fear—fear of The Man, fear of Mr. Charlie. Occasionally theirs is the irrational fear of something new and untested. But usually it is a highly rational emotion, the economic fear of losing your job, the physical fear of being shot at," volunteer Geoff Cowan wrote. "Public school teachers know they will be fired if they register to vote; so will domestic servants, so will factory workers, so will Negroes who live on plantations. In Mississippi registration is no private affair—

every week a list of newly registered voters is printed in the local newspaper." It was all well and good to talk about loyalty to the movement, but as voter registration workers discovered, loyalty often meant exposing one's family to dangers that would mean having to leave Mississippi. Charles Stewart found, "In house after house, the person would agree with me that he ought to register, but would point to his kids and tell me that he would no longer be able to support them if he tried to register."[19]

Soon it became commonplace for the volunteers doing voter registration to find themselves resenting the contradictory situations they faced. Volunteers who believed that sacrifices had to be made in order to bring about change invariably ran up against the defenses used by Mississippi blacks over the years to protect themselves. In such instances there was often a bitter edge to volunteer complaints about the pace of voter registration. "We did attempt to do some depressing work: bringing people down to the courthouse," a Gulfport volunteer wrote to her parents. "We had an appointment with about ten people to transport them down to register. But when we went to get them, they weren't home or they were busy or they didn't have their glasses. So after chasing around all day, we got no one, except one old man we had run into while asking directions."[20]

Not surprisingly, the voter registration workers most concerned about pressing ahead were especially prone to feeling discouraged when their canvassing or a meeting they had scheduled did not come off as planned. "They do not understand how politics works," Greenville volunteer Bill Hodes complained after a series of frustrating setbacks. "None of this is their fault. Mississippi has made damned sure that they don't know anything about politics, and even more sure that they are afraid. Nonetheless, it is frustrating, God it is frustrating, to have the people you are encouraging to become leaders lie to you and say that they cannot come to a meeting for this or that reason." In Clarksdale Charles Stewart used similar language to describe what he saw as the apathy of the black community. "If I were to characterize the Negro community in one word, it would be 'apathetic,'" he wrote. "This is really the most frightening thing about the whole situation, to see these masses of people, including many no older than myself, with their spirits crushed, just not seeming to care about anything."[21]

For the voter registration workers who directed their frustration inward, the tension was just as great. They ended up questioning their own motives and ability. Clarksdale volunteer Les Johnson wrote, "Canvassing is very trying. You walk down a little dusty street, with incredibly broken down shacks. The people sitting on porches staring away into nowhere. . . . I almost feel guilty, like I'm playing for numbers only." Nancy Jervis worried that all too often people listened to her and other volunteers because they were white. "We were playing on the racism of the society in order to overcome the racism of the society," she sadly concluded.[22]

What kept the voter registration workers going were individual acts of heroism they witnessed. In Drew it was a one-legged World War I veteran going to the courthouse to register. In Batesville it was a widow with ten children putting her job on the line to register. In McComb it was an entire voter registration class supporting one another. "The voter registration program, despite its shortcomings, is a beautiful thing to watch," a McComb worker observed. "The voter registration classes are slightly tense, but what is more present is hope, positiveness. The people dress up carefully, they shake each other's hands, await eagerly the return of those who have gone down to the courthouse already."[23]

It was nonetheless impossible for voter registration workers with their eyes open to ignore how often the people they took down to the courthouse never made it onto the voter rolls. Charles Rawlings's account of "grim and exhausted" applicants coming out of the Hattiesburg courthouse after being made to stand for two hours while taking the voter registration test is not unusual. Indeed, what is most striking about the letters and diaries of voter registration workers is their emphasis on the monotony and difficulty of the whole registration process. "Canvassing is dirty work. It is very tiring and frankly boring after the first hour or so," Bill Hodes observed. "Three hours is about all most people, including myself, can stand. It is almost impossible to overcome the fears of people, first at seeing a white man in their house, and then of course all the fears that the courthouse people make sure exist." In Holmes County Stephen Bingham described his day in equally grim terms: "And so it would go; each morning until late afternoon we would find ourselves trudging from house to house in the broad expanse of the Mississippi countryside, fighting off the heat, the dust, the discouragement, the fear, going from one dingy shack to the next. . . . Hard as it is to get a Negro to overcome his fears and attempt to register, it is even harder, once that Negro takes his test, for him to pass."[24]

For the most sensitive workers, those who put themselves in the shoes of the people they were asking to go to the courthouse, there were also questions that finally could not be answered. The more conscientiously these workers did their job, the more they worried about the burdens they were placing on others. "I could not help but wonder," volunteer Frank Cieciorka wrote, "how many citizens of San Jose would be willing to risk their jobs, their homes, even their lives, for the right to try to register to vote when they know they would probably fail the registration test."[25]

Before July ended, the volunteers had a clear sense of what they could and could not accomplish in Mississippi. They also knew that despite the FBI's search for the bodies of Schwerner, Chaney, and Goodman the federal government was going to provide them little practical help. It was a dose of reality many volunteers found difficult to accept, and it was compounded by heightened racial tensions on individual projects. Sometimes the tensions affected work; other times they created an atmosphere that prompted Vicksburg volunteer Patrick Thomas to describe two of his fellow volunteers as "Great White Fathers" who "spend three-fourths of their time condescending to the Southern Negro."[26]

Had the Summer Project been worth it, then? Or was the price—three missing, thirty-seven church burnings, thirty houses and buildings bombed, eighty beatings, and more than a thousand arrests—too high?[27] It was a question the volunteers could not help asking themselves, but in Mississippi there would be no room for a summing up. For the Summer Project leadership, the end of the summer was not a time for critique. It was a time for moving on to the final phase of the Summer Project—preparing the way for a delegation from the Mississippi Freedom Democratic party (MFDP) to go to the Democratic National Convention in Atlantic City and challenge the seating of the regular all-white Mississippi delegation.

The MFDP, which the Summer Project leadership had helped found earlier in the year, was no gimmick designed to divert attention from the long-range problems of black voter registration in Mississippi. Rather it was a way of taking a series of Mississippi issues and moving them from the local to the national level. The idea for the Atlantic City challenge had been planned well before the Summer Project. "We'll make a real effort on the floor of the Democratic convention to challenge the people Mississippi will send as a delegation to the convention in Atlantic City," Bob Moses told SNCC supporters at a New York fund-raiser in April. "The timetable on this will dovetail with the people coming down to

Mississippi for the summer." In March Moses had taken the first step toward making the Atlantic City challenge a reality. He had persuaded Joseph Rauh, Jr., general counsel for the United Auto Workers and a past president of the Americans for Democratic Action, to advise SNCC as to how to carry out the Atlantic City challenge. By May Rauh had agreed to write the MFDP's brief to the Democratic credentials committee and to represent the party at the convention.[28]

With Rauh the Summer Project organizers had what they could not supply from their own ranks—a consummate insider who had been fighting convention battles since 1948 when he helped write the first civil rights plank into the Democratic party platform. Now the organizers were free to concentrate on their preconvention strategy: put together an integrated MFDP; send black MFDP representatives to all the delegate-selection meetings of the regular Mississippi Democratic party; and, assuming the blacks would be barred from these meetings, argue that they were more faithful to the rules of the national Democratic party than the all-white Mississippi Democratic party. It was a sound strategy in every way. It gave a reason to organize in every county in Mississippi, and it put pressure on the national Democratic party to face up to the differences between what it espoused and what the Mississippi Democratic party (which in 1964 would end up supporting Republican Barry Goldwater) represented.[29]

On April 26, at a meeting at the Masonic Temple in Jackson, the Mississippi Freedom Democratic party was officially formed. Lawrence Guyot, a SNCC field secretary and native Mississippian, was elected chairman, and a twelve-member executive committee was chosen to decide policy until a permanent executive committee could be elected. The MFDP now had the official status it needed to begin the process that would take it to Atlantic City.[30]

On June 16, the day on which Democratic party precinct meetings were scheduled throughout Mississippi, blacks from

the MFDP made their first official attempt to become involved in the Mississippi Democratic party. As expected,
they found the party closed to them. Three-fourths of the
Democratic precincts never even bothered to hold delegation-
selection meetings; in those precincts that did, MFDP representatives were, with few exceptions, denied admittance or
limited to token participation. A week later, when MFDP
representatives attempted to attend the regular Democratic
party county conventions, they met still more barriers. Even
in towns where they had previously been allowed some
participation in meetings, they found themselves relegated to
the status of observers.[31]

The first stage of the Freedom party's Atlantic City
quest was over. The party had been rejected when it tried to
play by the Mississippi Democrats' delegate-selection rules.
Now it was free to steer an independent course and choose its
own delegates for Atlantic City. The second stage of the
MFDP's quest would not, however, prove easier than the
first. In selecting sixty-eight delegates and alternates for
Atlantic City, the MFDP was determined to get as large a
turnout as possible of black voters and to make sure that from
precinct to county level it followed the same rules which it
charged the Mississippi Democratic party with violating.

The MFDP's one advantage in July was that it could now
use volunteers from the Summer Project. In a July 19 memo
Bob Moses made it clear that for the rest of the summer the
Atlantic City challenge would be the Summer Project's chief
priority. "We *cannot* do everything at one time, and the
challenge, which we have committed ourselves to, is *by itself*
an overwhelming task for our limited staff," he declared in an
emergency memorandum. "*If it is done correctly, there will be
no time to do regular voter registration work.*"[32]

For the volunteers who had been doing regular voter
registration, the switch to MFDP registration was welcome.
"What I have been feeling for over a week now was just

confirmed by a long memo from Jackson. I don't think we should spend any more time taking people down to the courthouse to get spiritually bent down," Bill Hodes wrote to his parents. "Now we should put all our efforts into MFDP work, mainly getting voter registration forms filled out by the thousands." The reaction was similar elsewhere. "Voter registration has been stalled for over a week—the registrar has closed the courthouse," a Clarksdale volunteer noted. "The one bright spot is the Freedom Democratic Party."[33]

MFDP registration was not easy. In Greenwood whites beat up a volunteer doing MFDP work. In Hattiesburg the home of two MFDP leaders was bombed, and in Holly Springs the police surrounded a school where an MFDP precinct meeting was being held. Nonetheless, by comparison with regular voter registration, which meant a trip to the courthouse, MFDP registration had built-in advantages. It could be accomplished entirely within the black community—in churches, gas stations, beauty parlors, barber shops— and it could be done on a simple registration form rather than the complicated one used by Mississippi in its regular elections. Even the memories evoked by the MFDP campaign were good ones. They recalled the 1963 Freedom Vote, when Northern college students made their first large-scale appearance in Mississippi and more than eighty thousand blacks cast protest ballots on behalf of their candidates for governor and lieutenant governor.[34]

As the MFDP campaign went on, volunteers found themselves working more intensely and shaping their days so they were busiest when black workers were at home. "Reaching great numbers of people to fill out forms meant working longer, odder hours," Sally Belfrage noted. "Voter registration workers started getting up at sunrise and sleeping in midday, then making the rounds again at night." The response to the MFDP campaign made the extra effort seem worth it. While the distinction between registering for the

MFDP and registering at the courthouse caused some initial confusion, it went away quickly enough for most volunteers to be encouraged by the results of their canvassing. "Fear reigned at first—but soon people were excited about the prospects of the party and neighbors were talking to neighbors about the 'New Thing.' Block parties and mass meetings were being held many times a week in various parts of town," a Vicksburg volunteer reported. "They leaped at involvement with a process that has always worked against them," Walthall volunteer Christopher Wilson discovered, and in Columbus a volunteer was relieved to find, "The delegates were teachers, housewives, packinghouse workers, a toy factory worker, in short, a genuine cross-section of the community."[35]

Especially among the Summer Project staff there was a sense that the MFDP campaign was taking the summer in the direction it was supposed to go. "I was elated because it seemed that at last we were building the type of organization that I had long hoped for. It had a broad base among black people and a clear structure that fed into counties and then [back] into precincts," SNCC veteran James Forman observed. By August 6, when the MFDP gathered in Jackson to choose the sixty-eight delegates and alternates who would travel to Atlantic City, it was a very different Mississippi Freedom Democratic party from the one that had been founded in April. An estimated eighty thousand eligible black voters had registered for the MFDP, and the publicity over the Atlantic City challenge had begun to elicit support across the country. The Masonic Temple in Jackson was filled to capacity for the MFDP state convention. Among the delegates there was a feeling of hope, a sense of initiating change rather than waiting for it to happen. The setbacks of the Summer Project —the violence, the church burnings, the failures in voter registration—were now assets, grim proof of what blacks were up against in Mississippi and a claim upon the liberal conscience of the Democratic party.[36]

9

No Two Seats

As he watched the delegates from the Mississippi Freedom Democratic party board the buses that would take them from Jackson to the Democratic National Convention in Atlantic City, SNCC Executive Secretary James Forman felt uneasy. He had been one of the Summer Project organizers who believed it was important to challenge the "lily white" Mississippi Democratic party. But he also believed the challenge would be turned back. "I was concerned about the aftermath," Forman later wrote. "The challenge had to be

made, but we couldn't win in Atlantic City—how would the
people accept their defeat? Would they see their attempt as a
resistance effort in a long struggle or would they be discouraged and give up?"[1]

Forman was not alone in his concerns. But he knew that
this was not a time to focus on all that might go wrong in
Atlantic City. Among the MFDP delegates there was a sense
of optimism. As one put it shortly after the Jackson MFDP
convention ended, "Whether we're seated in Atlantic City or
not, we'll be there to tell the world that we are dissatisfied
with what is happening in Mississippi." It was not a naive
assessment. The MFDP did not have to pull off a miracle to
succeed in Atlantic City; it did not even have to win a
majority vote of the credentials committee. With eleven
votes—just 10 percent of the credentials committee—the
MFDP would gain the right to have its claims debated before
the full Democratic convention. After that, the support of only
eight states would require the convention to take a roll-call
vote to decide which Mississippi delegation should be seated.[2]

The possibility that the MFDP might succeed, or at least
score an enormous propaganda victory, was not lost on the
regular Mississippi Democratic party. On August 13, acting
on a request from the attorney general of Mississippi, a
Mississippi chancery court judge banned the MFDP on the
grounds that it represented a "conspiracy" which would
"cause irreparable damage to the public." Soon after, Lawrence Guyot, the MFDP's chairman, was arrested on charges
dating back to a January demonstration and ordered to begin
a thirty-day jail sentence which would make it impossible for
him to be in Atlantic City.[3]

"We seem to have the Mississippi delegation worried,"
a Laurel volunteer gleefully noted. "They have a court
injunction against the Mississippi Freedom Democratic party
and have been serving injunctions on all the local leaders
to keep them from participating." The greatest challenge to

the Mississippi regulars, however, came from an event that since June had been out of their hands—the disappearance of Michael Schwerner, James Chaney, and Andrew Goodman. Throughout the summer Mississippi officials and their defenders had repeatedly insisted there was no proof that the three men had in fact been murdered. One month after their disappearance, Mississippi Senator James Eastland had issued an angry press release declaring there was not "a shred of evidence" that the three civil rights workers were the victims of racial violence. "No one wants to charge that a hoax has been perpetrated, because there is too little evidence to show just what did happen," Eastland observed. "But as time goes on and the search continues, if some evidence is not produced, I think the people of America will be justified in considering other alternatives a more valid solution to the mystery, instead of accepting as true the accusation of the agitators that a heinous crime has been committed."[4]

On August 4 all such claims of innocence lost their credibility. At 8:15 that morning, armed with a search warrant quietly obtained the day before in Biloxi, the FBI began a search for the three missing civil rights workers on the Old Jolly Farm of Olen Burrage. In addition to heavy earthmoving equipment, agents brought along tarpaulins and army field rations—they were prepared for several days' search. But the tip they had gotten from their informant was accurate. The bodies were in the earthen dam that had just been constructed on Burrage's farm.

The FBI report of what happened next is as grim as it is precise. "At approximately 2:50 p.m. the pungent odor of decaying flesh was clearly discernible," the report notes. "Approximately one-quarter mile from the excavation site numerous vultures or buzzards were observed reconnoitering." By 3:00 p.m. "the heels and back portions of a pair of man's boots were observed." Then "a meticulous removal of the earth surrounding the boots revealed, at 3:18 p.m., the outline of a human body." It was Michael Schwerner. Two hours later the bodies of Andrew Goodman and James Chaney were recovered, and at 8:43 that night, after the families of the three men had been notified, FBI Director J. Edgar Hoover reported to the country what had happened.[5]

The headlines in the August 5 *New York Times* and in newspapers around the country were from Vietnam. Fighting between American destroyers and North Vietnamese PT boats had broken out in the Gulf of Tonkin. But the news from Vietnam did not long obscure what was happening in Mississippi. In the weeks following the discovery of the bodies, the nation increasingly saw the Mississippi that the Summer Project workers had seen in the forty-four days that Schwerner, Chaney, and Goodman were missing. Even in death the murdered men could not escape the power of Mississippi racism. An autopsy done on James Chaney at the request of the Summer Project organizers revealed that, contrary to what Mississippi officials had stated, Chaney had been badly beaten. "I have never witnessed bones so severely shattered, except in tremendously high-speed accidents such as airplane crashes," New York pathologist David Spain reported.[6]

In Greenville the liberal *Delta Democrat-Times* observed, "Now that the three missing civil rights workers have been found, brutally murdered, in Neshoba County, many of us in Mississippi need to take a long hard look at ourselves." But few in Mississippi were prepared to take such a look. In her memoir *Witness at Philadelphia* Florence Mars, one of the few whites in Neshoba County to say from the start that Schwerner, Chaney, and Goodman were murdered, describes how after the bodies were discovered most people tried to act as if nothing had happened. The reaction of Mississippi's politicians and newspapers to the news was far more brutal. They immediately went on the offensive against the state's Northern critics. "A new hate campaign against Mississippi is sure to follow the finding of the bodies of the three civil rights workers near Philadelphia," the *Meridian Star* complained. "The liberals will outdo themselves to find words vicious enough to use in vilifying every man, woman, and child in Mississippi en masse." As far as the *Meridian Star* was concerned, it was the Summer Project workers who were to blame for initiating the violence that led to the murders. "We know that, no matter who the murderers are, the 'civil rights' organizations share the blame, inasmuch as they care nothing for how much violence they provoke. We know that we are eminently decent people who can be proud of our state," the *Star* declared. But not only newspapers like the *Star* took the offensive. Although the principal suspects in the triple murder were the sheriff and deputy sheriff of Neshoba County (they and nineteen others would be arrested by the FBI in December), Mississippi officials continued to insist that outsiders, not Mississippians, failed to understand the significance of the three deaths.[7]

At the Neshoba County Fair, which began in Philadelphia the week after the bodies of Schwerner, Chaney, and Goodman were discovered, Governor Paul Johnson struck the note of defiance that white Mississippi would take in the coming months. In a speech which attracted national attention, Governor Johnson told a fair crowd of six thousand that neither Mississippians nor state officials had any obligations to obey the new Civil Rights Act of 1964. "Integration is like prohibition, if people don't want it, a whole army can't enforce it," Johnson warned. "People who want to enforce integration in Mississippi had better think nine hundred thousand times." From Johnson came no expression of sympathy for the families of the dead civil rights workers, nor was there a pledge that the state would do its best to find their murderers. "The white people of Mississippi know that the vast majority of colored people of this state have turned their backs on the motley crew of invaders of our state,"

Johnson declared. "We will not permit outsiders to subvert our people and our rights."[8]

Anyone who doubted that Governor Johnson spoke for the Mississippi political establishment had only to compare his Neshoba County Fair speech with the statement issued by the Mississippi Democratic party at its state convention. As the Mississippi regulars made clear, they did not intend to change just because federal law had changed. "We oppose, condemn, and deplore the Civil Rights Act of 1964," the Mississippi regulars announced. "We believe in the separation of the races in all phases of our society. It is our belief that the separation of the races is necessary for the peace and tranquility of all the people of Mississippi and the continuing good relationship which has existed over the years."[9]

Within the Summer Project, especially among the staff, there was little surprise when the bodies of Schwerner, Chaney, and Goodman were found. There was, however, great doubt that the guilty parties would ever be charged for the murders, let alone tried and convicted. Among Northern supporters of civil rights it was shock, not battle fatigue, that marked the reaction to the discovery of the bodies. Liberal Democrats rallied to the MFDP's side. By early August nine state delegations and more than two dozen Democratic congressmen, including William F. Ryan of New York, Philip Burton of California, and Robert Kastenmeier of Wisconsin, had announced their support of the MFDP challenge. "I have just spent a week in Mississippi as a volunteer attorney," Ed Koch, the future mayor of New York and then a reform leader in New York, wrote to David Lawrence, chairman of the Democratic National Convention credentials committee. "From personal observations I know there is no justice in Laurel or personal safety in Mississippi. The state of Mississippi is a police state rivaling Nazi Germany," Koch declared in a telegram urging the seating of the Freedom Democratic party.[10]

Five days before the convention was due to begin, the *New York Times* endorsed a compromise that made room for both Mississippi delegations. "The seating of both delegations, each with a half vote, would seem a sensible middle ground," the *Times* suggested. "Until the president works out a comparable settlement, he will stand open to the charge that he chose silence in order to compete more effectively with his Republican opponent for Southern white racist votes."[11]

Could such momentum carry the Freedom party to victory? "We really thought with all the efforts that had gone into the summer—with black Mississippi citizens having made such a statement—the Freedom party couldn't possibly be denied," volunteer Pat Vail remembered thinking. But even among SNCC veterans it did not seem unreasonable to hope. "Initially I thought we would go down in defeat," SNCC field secretary Hollis Watkins believed. "But then based on the response that had come from other parts of the country and those in Congress, I felt we would be victorious." On Saturday, August 22, two days before the convention was scheduled to open, Fannie Lou Hamer provided the first indication of what the MFDP could do when it got a chance to make its case. Testifying before the credentials committee in a room that MFDP attorney Joseph Rauh, Jr., had made sure would accommodate the television cameras of the three networks, Hamer stunned not only the committee members but a nationwide audience with her account of what happened to her in Winona, Mississippi, after she was arrested by police for attending a voter registration workshop.[12]

"It wasn't too long before three white men came to my cell. One of these men was a state highway patrolman,"

Hamer told the committee. "He said, 'We are going to make you wish you was dead.'

"I was carried out of that cell into another cell where they had two Negro prisoners. The state highway patrolman ordered the first Negro to take the blackjack.

"The first Negro prisoner ordered me, by orders from the state highway patrolman for me, to lay down on a bunk bed on my face, and I laid on my face.

"The first Negro began to beat, and I was beat by the first Negro until he was exhausted, and I was holding my hands behind me at the time on my left side because I suffered from polio when I was six years old.

"After the first Negro had beat until he was exhausted, the state highway patrolman ordered the second Negro to take the blackjack.

"The second Negro began to beat and I began to work my feet, and the state highway patrolman ordered the first Negro who had beat to set on my feet to keep me from working my feet. I began to scream and one white man got up and began to beat me in my head and tell me to hush.

"... All of this is on account we want to register, to become first-class citizens."[13]

There was nothing the regular Mississippi delegates could do to match Mrs. Hamer's story. E. K. Collins, head of the Mississippi delegation, argued that he and those who had come with him to Atlantic City had been "elected in the free exercise of their democratic prerogatives under the laws of our state." But compared with Hamer, Collins did not elicit much sympathy. His testimony, like his insistence that Rita Schwerner, the widow of Michael Schwerner, should not be allowed to speak before the credentials committee because she was not a Mississippian, came across as cold-blooded and legalistic.[14]

The networks, anxious to get a story out of the convention that did not seem like managed news, were not the only ones to realize the power of Hamer's testimony. In Washington Lyndon Johnson was panicked by it. From his point of view, it was too good. The president did not want the MFDP credentials battle to escalate to the point where the Mississippi regulars, then the entire South, bolted the convention. In an effort to blunt the impact of Hamer's testimony, the president called a news conference while she was still speaking, and the television audience watching her live never heard the end of her testimony. The president's advantage was brief, however. That night on the evening news the networks replayed Hamer's testimony, and the nation heard and saw what the White House had hoped would remain behind closed doors.[15]

The fall elections would provide Johnson with a landslide 15.9-million-vote margin over Republican Barry Goldwater, securing Democrats their largest majority in the Senate since 1943 and their largest majority in the House since 1939. But at this moment the president was driven by fear. He had no sense that he could look forward to such a triumph. Although he had pushed for quick passage of the Civil Rights Act of 1964 and would later steer the Voting Rights Act of 1965 through Congress, Johnson was worried about losing a South in which 64 percent of white voters were Democrats. "I've just been over to see the president, and we agreed that the backlash created by the Freedom party is going to cost Johnson the election," Joseph Rauh was warned by his longtime friend and employer, United Auto Workers President Walter Reuther, just before the Democratic Convention began. Reuther may have been exaggerating in order to impress Rauh, but the president's worry was genuine. He believed, as he told his aide Bill Moyers, that he needed a big victory in November to push his Great Society programs through Congress, and he was convinced that the key to a big victory was making sure his civil rights commitment did not drive away moderate white voters.[16]

Saturday's triumph proved to be the high point of the MFDP's Atlantic City campaign. What the MFDP needed to advance its cause—eleven credentials committee votes and eight state delegations—was not something that Fannie Lou Hamer's story or the sacrifices of the summer could provide. The MFDP now depended on its ability to lobby for votes and the skill of its counsel Joseph Rauh in countering White House pressure for a quick settlement of the Mississippi question. It was a contest neither the MFDP nor the Summer Project staff and volunteers were equipped to win. "I was at the convention and in a lot of backroom meetings," SNCC veteran Frank Smith recalled. "Almost from the day we got there, we lost control of the negotiating process."[17]

The discomforts of the run-down and air-conditionless Gem Hotel, where the MFDP delegation was housed in Atlantic City, could be suffered; but other disadvantages could not be overcome. There was no way the MFDP could know as much about the administration's strategy as the administration could know about MFDP strategy. As a Senate Committee to Study Governmental Operations later discovered, during the convention the FBI placed listening devices in Martin Luther King's hotel rooms and in SNCC's storefront office and in the agency's own words kept the White House "fully apprised of all major developments in the convention's course." The president could count on knowing the MFDP's strategy and the advice it was getting from friendly senators, representatives, and governors. Most important, there was no way, except for moral suasion, the MFDP could compete with the White House for delegate support. From judgeships to federal appointments, the administration had everything it needed to persuade wavering delegates.[18]

On the boardwalk in front of the convention hall, many of the volunteers who had come to Atlantic City began a vigil on behalf of MFDP. Other volunteers, along with the Summer Project organizers, tried to lobby anyone they knew. But from Sunday to Tuesday, most of the meetings that would decide the MFDP fate were ones they never attended. As volunteer Sally Belfrage wrote in her *Freedom Summer*, "We had exhausted our supply of tensions in a confrontation with Southern reality, and now were flung with no transition into the world of deals and decisions, ulcers and dexedrine, funny hats and red, white, and blue—expected to participate, to be political. The set of our responses was wrong—a case of coming hungry to a meal that in the first chew turns to painted plaster, and lacking the manners to swallow it anyway."[19]

On Sunday morning the MFDP began the frustrating process of trying to make headway against the White House. The plan floated by the administration for resolving the Mississippi question was told to Rauh by Harold Leventhal, general counsel for the Democratic National Committee. Leventhal, who six months later would be named by the president to the U.S. Court of Appeals for the District of Columbia Circuit, was, as Rauh put it, one of the administration's "hatchet men." The proposal he passed on reflected the White House belief that its best strategy was to be very tough on the MFDP. The president's plan required the Mississippi regulars, most of whom were Goldwater backers, to pledge their support to the Democratic ticket. It offered the MFDP fraternal seating (but no votes) on the convention floor, and it guaranteed that the party would investigate the problem of segregated delegations. Rauh's public response to this proposal—the "back-of-the-bus" plan, as the MFDP called it— was to reject it. "We will accept nothing but equal representation with the regular Democrats," he told the press. "Both delegations should be seated and the vote split, or both should be barred."[20]

Rauh was not being naive; he realized he was fighting

"the whole Democratic political machine." But his aim was not the kind of victory that would put the president, whom he supported, in a box. In Rauh's earlier talks with the White House, presidential aides had agreed that the easiest way out of the Mississippi problem, given the fact that there would be no controversial votes at the convention, would be to seat both delegations. Congresswoman Edith Green, a member of the credentials committee, had also floated a dual-seating compromise ("We would have accepted the Green proposal," Fannie Lou Hamer later acknowledged), and Rauh expected that on Sunday afternoon, when the credentials committee got down to hard bargaining, the debate would center on the Johnson plan versus the dual-seating plan.[21]

But at the Sunday credentials committee meeting neither Rauh nor Green ever had a chance to offer dual-seating plans. The first person recognized by committee chairman David Lawrence was a delegate from Wyoming who offered the administration's plan. Then, as Rauh and Green raised their hands for recognition, Lawrence turned instead to Green's Oregon colleague, Congressman Al Ullman, who proposed a marginal improvement on the White House plan: the MFDP should be given two at-large votes, not just fraternal seating.[22]

For Rauh, Ullman's proposal came as a complete shock. Ullman was one of the credentials committee members whom Rauh was counting on to side with the MFDP. Now he was proposing a variation on the administration's back-of-the-bus offer. Rauh and the MFDP were caught in a bind. According to Democratic party rules, the credentials committee could consider only one proposal and one substitute. "There was no further parliamentary way you could get anything else. We were stymied at the moment," Rauh acknowledged. As the meeting wore on, it was apparent that neither the MFDP nor the Johnson administration was prepared to make further concessions. Finally Walter Mondale, then attorney general of Minnesota, proposed that a five-member subcommittee deal with the Mississippi question. The credentials committee readily assented, happy to have the Mississippi issue taken from its hands and deposited with a group that could function in private.[23]

Sunday's credentials committee meeting was a setback for the MFDP, but that night, after a strategy session in Martin Luther King's rooms, Rauh, Moses, and other MFDP supporters remained optimistic. In Monday's papers the MFDP's confidence was reflected in Aaron Henry, its delegation chairman, declaring, "We can go home to Mississippi and look down from the balcony to see how things are going. We did not come to Atlantic City to get the same kind of back-of-the-bus treatment we have gotten in Mississippi." Even without Al Ullman the MFDP had more than enough votes to get a minority report out of the credentials committee and placed before the entire Democratic convention.[24]

The White House assessment of the MFDP's support was the same as Rauh's, and on Sunday evening a worried president became more directly involved in negotiations. Tom Finney, a law partner of White House adviser Clark Clifford and one of the men who had accompanied Allen Dulles to Mississippi after the disappearance of Schwerner, Chaney, and Goodman, was assigned to work full time on the Mississippi question, and Hubert Humphrey, who was in Atlantic City actively seeking the vice-presidential nomination, was asked to become involved as well.[25]

Monday morning, during an MFDP rally at the Union Temple Baptist Church, Rauh received a call to meet that afternoon with Humphrey in his rooms at the Pageant Motel, the administration's Atlantic City headquarters. The Monday meeting was the first of several with Humphrey, a longtime civil rights supporter whose vice-presidential nomination, Johnson aides let it be known, now depended on his ability to bring about a peaceful solution to the Mississippi question. The meeting in Humphrey's rooms included Rauh, Bob

Moses, Martin Luther King, and pro-MFDP credentials committee members Edith Green and Robert Kastenmeier. The
administration was directly represented by Humphrey and
Tom Finney and indirectly by Walter Mondale, a Humphrey
protégé and the leading candidate to fill out his term in the
Senate if Humphrey received the vice-presidential post. By
the end of the two-hour meeting, no one's political fortunes
had improved. As Rauh observed, "Everything was dis-
cussed and nothing happened." As long as the administration's and Ullman's proposals were the only options before
the MFDP, it was clear that no settlement would be reached.
The meeting produced a bitter exchange between Humphrey
and Bob Moses over who spoke for black Mississippi, and
later Edith Green and Humphrey clashed so bitterly that
Green left the meeting and went before television cameras to
say that Humphrey was trying to force the Freedom party into
a sellout.[26]

The administration's only choice was to put off a show-
down with the MFDP. Late Monday afternoon credentials
committee chairman David Lawrence announced that a final
decision on Mississippi would be postponed until Tuesday.
Rauh's public response was to insist that the MFDP was as
determined as ever. "We can win on the floor. I think we're
going the whole distance," he told reporters. But privately
Rauh was worried. As negotiations dragged on, the White
House began putting tremendous pressure on pro-MFDP
delegates, promising jobs to some, threatening others with
the loss of appointments they had been expecting. Rauh
could see his delegate support on the credentials committee
eroding. Equally serious from Rauh's point of view, delegates
who were prepared to speak out for the MFDP on the convention floor were also being silenced. Liberal Illinois Senator
Paul Douglas, who in July had proposed seating both Mississippi delegations, now let Rauh know that he was no longer
prepared to challenge the president.[27]

As Tuesday began it was nonetheless the White House that made the first move to break the Mississippi deadlock. On Monday night the president phoned Walter Reuther, then in contract negotiations with General Motors, and prevailed on him to come to Atlantic City to act as a mediator with Rauh and the MFDP. As the head of the union for which Rauh was general counsel, and a longtime financial supporter of the civil rights movement, Reuther was ideally suited to represent the president. To bolster his position, Reuther brought with him Bayard Rustin, now at the height of his influence because of his successful organization of the March on Washington. After a Tuesday breakfast meeting with Mondale, Humphrey, Lawrence, and Finney, Reuther became the principal spokesman for the final administration proposal— "a Godfather offer," Rauh would call it—to the MFDP.[28]

The offer consisted of five points: (1) The MFDP would receive two at-large seats. (2) Aaron Henry, the MFDP delegation chairman, and the Reverend Ed King, white chaplain of Tougaloo College and Henry's running mate in the Freedom Vote of 1963, would fill the two seats. (3) The remaining MFDP delegates would be treated as guests of the convention. (4) Only the Mississippi Democratic party delegates willing to take a loyalty oath to support the Democratic presidential nominee would be seated. (5) A committee would be appointed to make certain that all future delegations to the Democratic National Convention were chosen regardless of race, creed, or national origin.[29]

The White House hoped its plan would be adequate to prevent most of the Southern states from bolting the convention and at the same time satisfy the MFDP as a step in the right direction. But the administration was not about to leave acceptance of its offer to chance; it was determined to give the MFDP little opportunity for maneuvering. Late Tuesday morning Walter Mondale called together his credentials subcommittee to gain its approval of the White House plan. The plan was endorsed 3 to 2, with the two Southerners on the committee dissenting but promising they would still do their best to prevent a Southern walkout. Mondale's only remaining problem was now the credentials committee itself. The task of dealing with Rauh, who would be arguing the MFDP's case when the credentials committee met in the afternoon, was assigned to Walter Reuther.[30]

As Rauh was heading into the Tuesday credentials committee meeting, he was stopped by Congressman Charles Diggs and told to call Reuther. Their conversation, Rauh recalled, was a short one in which Reuther made it clear he was speaking both for the White House and as Rauh's employer. "This is the decision," Rauh would remember Reuther saying. "They are going to exclude the Mississippi people unless they take an oath, which they said they won't take. So they're being excluded. They're going to give you two delegates, so you've won that. They're going to give you a pledge that they'll never seat lily-white delegates again. So you've won this. This is a tremendous victory, and I want you to take it."[31]

Convinced that the White House would go no further, Rauh was prepared to carry Reuther's message back to the MFDP. He thought the administration's choice of Aaron Henry and Ed King rather than Aaron Henry and Fannie Lou Hamer was a political mistake, but he was nonetheless ready to do what he could to get the offer accepted. Rauh could not make a commitment on his own; before the convention he and Aaron Henry had agreed to consult on all key decisions. Rauh also knew that as pressure mounted for a compromise, the MFDP delegates and Summer Project staff were increasingly suspicious of him. That morning, when he pleaded for understanding of the position his friend Hubert Humphrey had been put in, Rauh had been severely criticized by angry MFDP delegates, and in the Tuesday *Washington Post* he had been singled out for trying to serve too many interests. Next to a story headlined, "Clash of Rauh's Convention Roles Hints Trouble with Administration," the *Post* ran a cartoon showing Rauh as a chariot driver trying to control five horses. Four of the horses had names: Atlantic City Convention, Labor, ADA, Mississippi Freedom Democrats. The fifth wore a ten-gallon cowboy hat.[32]

As it turned out, Rauh never got a chance to check with Aaron Henry and the MFDP delegation. As he entered the credentials committee room, Rauh asked Mondale for time to consult with the MFDP, but the word from the White House was that there would be no more delays. Rauh could only try to stall, hoping that he could somehow gain the time he needed to consult with the MFDP. But the credentials committee was not about to listen to Rauh any longer nor agree to the roll-call vote he wanted on the Mississippi question. Walter Mondale's presentation of the administration's offer made it seem like a triumph for the MFDP, an acknowledgment by a sympathetic White House of what Mondale called "a clear pattern of discrimination and intimidation" in Mississippi. By a voice vote the credentials committee approved the White House plan. Rauh and those still loyal to the MFDP held their ground, but the damage was done. Rauh no longer had the eleven votes needed to file a minority report. Mondale's presentation and White House pressure had reduced the MFDP's support on the credentials committee to eight delegates.[33]

Meanwhile, the White House was continuing its pressure on other fronts. As the credentials committee was meeting at convention hall, Reuther and Humphrey were meeting with Moses, Ed King, Aaron Henry, Bayard Rustin, and Martin Luther King, among others, in Humphrey's rooms. The MFDP representatives in the room had been told of the administration's final offer, and as the meeting wore on they were, despite their anger, trying to find a way out of the situation. Ed King believed that if the two delegates the

MFDP was offered could be split into four half-delegates—to include Aaron Henry, Fannie Lou Hamer, Victoria Gray, and himself—the MFDP might accept the White House plan. "We had," King recalled, "just about, I felt, gotten Humphrey to the point where we would have an hour or so to go talk to the delegation [about a new compromise] when an aide rushed into the hotel room and said to Humphrey, 'You must come look at TV.'" There on the screen was Walter Mondale announcing that the credentials committee had voted in favor of the administration's two-seat plan. For Bob Moses in particular, the announcement was startling. He had not assumed that Reuther and Humphrey would come around to the MFDP's point of view, but he had assumed they were serious in discussing possible variations on the White House plan. Now the Tuesday afternoon negotiations seemed like nothing more than a crude deception, a trick to isolate the MFDP and SNCC leadership while the credentials committee passed the Mississippi plan the White House wanted.[34]

Ed King later said that when the credentials committee settlement was announced on television, Hubert Humphrey looked shocked. "I felt that even Humphrey had been used by the president," King concluded. Whether Humphrey was a participant or a pawn in the White House's maneuvering, the MFDP's dilemma was the same. In the time that remained before the evening session of the convention, there was no way the MFDP could regain the delegate support it had lost, or effectively counter the impression that Walter Mondale had made with his television announcement that the credentials committee had amicably settled the Mississippi question.[35]

That night, when Joseph Rauh returned to the convention hall he was congratulated by most of the delegates he saw for achieving a "great victory" over the Mississippi Democratic party. Save for three of their delegates, the Mississippi regulars had left the convention rather than accept that part of the credentials committee settlement requiring them to pledge their support to the Democratic presidential ticket. "Mississippi's debt to the national Democratic party is now paid in full, and we stand tonight—as a state, as a people, and as a member of an organized political group—absolutely free of all obligations, all old ties, and all debts," Governor Paul Johnson announced in a special television broadcast from Jackson. But on Tuesday afternoon, as the MFDP delegates gathered at the Union Temple Baptist Church, they were in no mood to celebrate the departure of the Mississippi regulars. They felt betrayed not only by the Democratic party but by Joseph Rauh, whom they had counted on to make their case.[36]

After days of witnessing events they could not control, the MFDP delegates were now in a position to decide their own fate—yet their options were narrower than at any time since the convention began. The only question left for the MFDP delegates to decide was how they should respond to the compromise plan the White House had forced on them. Should they go along with the compromise, treating it, as so many of their liberal supporters urged, as a political breakthrough? Or should they vote their feelings and reject the compromise as tokenism? After a hurried discussion, the Freedom party voted to reject the compromise. That evening, at the urging of Bob Moses, MFDP delegates carried their protest into the convention hall. Using passes supplied to them by friendly delegates from other states, they slipped into the seats left by the Mississippi regulars. Sympathetic visitors in the gallery began shouting, "Freedom now," and for a while it appeared there would be a struggle on the convention floor to remove the MFDP delegates. But on orders from the president, who had already been upstaged by the MFDP more than he liked, the sergeants at arms withdrew, leaving the MFDP in control of the Mississippi section.[37]

The compromise question, however, was still unresolved for the MFDP delegates. Anxious that the delegates hear in detail the arguments for accepting the White House compromise, Aaron Henry called for a Wednesday meeting at the Union Temple Baptist Church. Henry wanted the MFDP to accept the two seats it was offered, and he hoped that the anger of the day before might have subsided enough for the administration's plan to seem more appealing. He arranged for a series of speakers to address the MFDP, and then for the delegates to take a second vote on the White House offer. Most of the speakers Henry had lined up—from Bayard Rustin to Martin Luther King to Senator Wayne Morse—either favored or leaned toward the compromise. In the wake of the credentials committee battle, none of them claimed that the MFDP had gotten all it deserved. Rather, their argument was that the MFDP would benefit from a Johnson administration and a Democratic party with which it was on good terms. Bayard Rustin argued that the time had come for the MFDP to make the transition from protest to politics. The only way the MFDP could take that step, Rustin insisted, was to show its allies in the Democratic party that it wanted their help. The theme was one that Martin Luther King continued, arguing that Hubert Humphrey had told him there would be "a new day in Mississippi" if the White House offer were accepted. The president would, King assured the delegates, give the MFDP the White House meeting it had been seeking.[38]

While Bayard Rustin was speaking, SNCC field secretary Mendy Samstein became so angry that he shouted from the audience, "You're a traitor, Bayard, a traitor! Sit down!" Samstein was quickly silenced by others in SNCC, but it was clear that his anger reflected the feelings of most of the

Summer Project organizers and most of the MFDP delegates. They were in no mood to abandon their stance of the day before or to be charitable toward allies who were not prepared to back them all the way. Uppermost in their minds was the belief that in creating the MFDP they had, as one SNCC field secretary later observed, "followed each and every rule, each and every step, as the country and the party said it should be followed."[39]

Of all those who addressed the MFDP delegates on Wednesday, James Forman, SNCC's veteran executive secretary and an opponent of the compromise offer, came closest to summing up their mood. "You came not to be received as guests. You came to take regular seats to the convention. To accept the status of guests is to deny the legitimacy, the rightness of your position," Forman told the delegates. Then he went on to ask, "What effect will a decision to accept the honored guest status and the two seats-at-large, with the delegates named for you—what effect will this have upon your friends and your relatives and your fellow workers in the state of Mississippi?"[40]

The delegates knew the answer to Forman's question. Although they would return to Mississippi and work hard for the Johnson-Humphrey ticket, they were not about to accept a compromise that they believed trivialized the sacrifices they had made to come to Atlantic City. Earlier in the week, at a meeting held at the Deauville Hotel for all the black delegates, MFDP Secretary Annie Devine had answered longtime Chicago Congressman William Dawson's call to support the Democratic leadership by reminding him that the MFDP had its own priorities. "We have been treated like beasts in Mississippi. They shot us down like animals," Devine told a stunned Dawson. "We risk our lives coming up here." Now others stepped in to counter the advice they were getting from "all the big fish."[41]

Fannie Lou Hamer, who later observed that "everybody

that would compromise in five minutes is the people with a real good education," gave the most dramatic answer to the White House's offer. "We didn't come all this way for no two seats," she declared. Victoria Gray, who would run for Congress on the MFDP ticket, was no less "incensed" with the compromise offer, and like the overwhelming majority of MFDP delegates she had an easy time saying no to the White House. "I knew what we were asking for was in no way unwarranted. The peculiarity was that we were trying to achieve what everybody else in the country had done in just a few years," she recalled. "I was one of the people who was quite clear on the fact that we didn't need two seats at large. There was never any doubt where my vote was going."[42]

That evening Bob Moses and a group of MFDP delegates returned to the convention hall and once again occupied the section reserved for Mississippi. But the fallout from their rejection of the White House compromise continued beyond the convention. "We got more than anybody dreamed of," Joseph Rauh said of the MFDP's Atlantic City challenge, and among SNCC's and the MFDP's liberal allies there was a growing sense that Rauh spoke the truth. In liberal circles the MFDP's rejection of the White House offer was proof that the party did not know how the game of politics was played, and that SNCC was now on a course in which, as Allard Lowenstein, one of the architects of the 1963 Freedom Vote campaign, later put it, "You're either a true believer or a sellout."[43]

The growing liberal criticism of the MFDP and SNCC position was reflected in an Anthony Lewis story, "The Negro and Politics," which appeared in the August 27 *New York Times*. Lewis's assumption was that "the Freedom party's claims would have been brushed aside at any previous convention because of their legal "insubstantiality," and that "in this framework the credentials committee compromise appeared a remarkable victory for the Freedom group." What worried Lewis was that the MFDP had been so traumatized by the racism of Mississippi that it could not understand its own achievement. "It is plainly difficult for those long deprived of the most elementary rights to move from the first actions of demonstrations to the necessarily slowed and often more frustrating business of exerting influence by means of the vote and other political action," Lewis wrote, before going on to conclude, "The liberal concern is that a failure of the civil rights movement to accept the ambiguities and frustrations of politics—a decision to go on demonstrating instead—could have dangerous consequences in the long run."[44]

The harshest criticisms came from liberals within the civil rights movement itself. "You're trying to pluck defeat out of the jaws of victory," Bayard Rustin declared when the MFDP's final course of action at Atlantic City became clear, and by early 1965 he would spell out what he had in mind in his essay "From Protest to Politics: The Future of the Civil Rights Movement." There Rustin repeated his charge that the "FDP made a tactical error in spurning the compromise." In the future, he argued, the civil rights movement must shape its strategy around the forging of coalitions. "We need allies," Rustin insisted. "The future of the Negro struggle depends on whether the contradictions of this society can be resolved by a coalition of progressive forces which becomes the *effective* political majority in the United States."[45]

Even more outspoken in his criticism of the MFDP's action was NAACP Executive Secretary Roy Wilkins, whose organization had frequently clashed with SNCC over the best means to register black voters in the South. In a September 5 newspaper column, "Lost Victory in AC," Wilkins asked, "Did the Mississippi Freedom party delegates make the right choice in rejecting the compromise offer which would have seated two of their men as delegates-at-large in the Democratic National Convention in Atlantic City? If the objective was to throw out the entire Mississippi delegation and to seat, in its stead, the entire Freedom party delegation, then the decision of the leaders is understandable," Wilkins wrote. But that was not, Wilkins argued, the crux of the Mississippi seating question. What made the seating question important was that it provided a way of placing Mississippi "before the bar of public opinion" and forcing the Democratic party and the country to acknowledge that Mississippi's political institutions were racist. That happened in Atlantic City, Wilkins declared, but the MFDP was not able to recognize its victory. "The proof of that victory was the offer made to it, a signal of the revolution that had taken place. But the leaders of the Freedom party failed to read the sign. They are working diligently and sacrificially in the Negro revolution, but they could not recognize victory when it appeared."[46]

By contrast, especially among SNCC's veteran organizers, events in Atlantic City showed that coalitions posed a threat to the civil rights movement in Mississippi. "The big shock to me was to see how people who had committed themselves verbally were retracting and backing up from their commitment," Mississippi field secretary Hollis Watkins recalled. "Offering the two seats was a slap in the face. It was like you coming to my door and saying, 'Hollis, I'm hungry. Will you give me a plate of food?' And then my saying, 'I'm not going to give it you.' But then when I see the look on your face, I say on second thought, 'Take this grape.'" Julian Bond, SNCC's director of communications, remembered events the same way. "The fantastic compromise . . . wasn't a compromise. It was a sellout, and for a lot of people that was just the last straw," Bond recalled. "Political liberals in the party that SNCC had always counted on for support, under that kind of pressure, just couldn't

stand up to it. They wilted away." His thoughts were echoed
with even more finality by James Forman. "Atlantic City was
a powerful lesson, not only for black people from Mississippi
but for all of SNCC and many other people as well," Forman
wrote. "No longer was there any hope, among those who
still had it, that the federal government would change the
situation in the Deep South. The fine line of distinction
between the state governments and the federal government,
which we had used to build a movement, was played out."[47]

Looking back on the Atlantic City convention from the
perspective of the racial turmoil of the 1990s, Bob Moses
observed that if the Democratic party had come down on the
side of the Freedom Democrats, it would have been possible
to argue in the North as well as in the South that the MFDP's
kind of coalition-building was the promise of the future. "It
was a real watershed," Moses recalled. "The message could
have been, Work out your differences on the political front."
Moses was not being utopian in his thinking. The Democratic
party was in a position both to win the 1964 presidential
election *and* offer the MFDP a genuine compromise. Instead
the Democratic convention dealt a fatal blow to the arguments that Moses and Fannie Lou Hamer had advanced in
late 1963 on behalf of an interracial Summer Project and civil
rights movement. No longer were they in a position to refute
a Stokely Carmichael when he pointed to the treatment that
the MFDP had received and declared, "This proves that the
liberal Democrats are just as racist as Goldwater." As Carmichael later observed, after Atlantic City those who disagreed with him had "nowhere to go." Nor would it matter
that as a result of the Atlantic City compromise no state
delegation to a Democratic National Convention would ever
again be all white or that in 1968 the credentials committee
would bar the regular Mississippi delegation by an 84 to 10
vote, seating an integrated delegation in its place. In the
volatile context of 1964, the Summer Project leadership was

not looking that far down the road or even trusting that the language of the Mississippi compromise would be implemented.[48]

"Atlantic City in August 1964 was a place of happy, surging crowds and thunderous cheers," Lyndon Johnson wrote in his presidential memoir *The Vantage Point*. A more misleading summation is difficult to imagine. The 1964 Democratic convention in Atlantic City was a watershed for the civil rights movement. Especially among a younger generation of SNCC field secretaries, there was a sense that a new era had begun and that they were more on their own than ever. "The national Democratic party's rejection of the MFDP at the 1964 convention was to the civil rights movement what the Civil War was to American history: afterward, things could never be the same," observed Cleveland Sellers, a Mississippi field secretary, who in a year's time would become program director of SNCC. "Never again were we lulled into believing that our task was exposing injustices so that the 'good' people of America could eliminate them. We left Atlantic City with the knowledge that the movement had turned into something else."[49]

10

Loose Ends

Days before the Democratic National Convention, Summer Project organizers were looking ahead to fall in Mississippi as a small-scale version of summer. "In effect, the Mississippi Summer Project is never going to end," John Lewis declared in an August 19 letter asking the White House for more federal protection. "From now on people from all over the country will work in Mississippi to see that full human rights come to all its citizens." Publicly the Summer Project leadership was equally specific about its plans. "We asked those who wanted to remain in Mississippi this winter to sign up," Bob Moses told the *New Orleans Times-Picayune*, "and we were very surprised that 200 of them said they would stay."[1]

There was good reason to be hopeful about the fall. As they departed for Mississippi in June, Bob Moses had cautioned the volunteers, "Our goals are limited. If we can go and come back alive, then that is something." By August it was clear that the Summer Project staff and volunteers had done much more than go and come back alive. They had forced immediate passage of the 1964 Civil Rights Act. They had involved the press and the FBI in Mississippi as never before. And they had demonstrated that no area in the South was off limits for the civil rights movement.[2]

By September, just weeks after the Democratic National Convention, it was, however, as if all the preconvention talk about extending the Summer Project had been propaganda. SNCC, which with the end of summer was now meeting on its own most of the time, without the other organizations that made up COFO, was seeing the future very differently from the way it had only a month earlier. At the national level the focus of SNCC's doubts was the leadership of the Democratic party, but within Mississippi SNCC's chief worry was the volunteers from the Summer Project.

Tension between project staff and volunteers it had recruited was not new. From the start the staff had worried about being upstaged and allowing its strategy to be dictated by the media's fascination with the volunteers. A number of volunteers, as their journals and letters show, were not above patronizing the staff, and even when they didn't mean to, the volunteers could produce hurt feelings. "You got these girls from Radcliffe, Wellesley, Berkeley, coming down, very articulate, and boys, too," SNCC's director of communications, Julian Bond, recalled, "and they'd come into a situation and take it over—not always because they were patronizing, but sometimes simply because they were more skilled."

Worse still, Bond found, there were times when whites could get results that blacks could not. "A black civil rights worker would come up to an elderly Negro man and say, 'We want you to go down and register to vote, sir.' And he'd say, 'Well no, I don't think I can. . . .' But you get a young white kid to come up and say, 'Mister Smith, we want you to go register to vote,' and he'd say, 'Oh, yessuh, Cap'n, yessuh, yessuh, be right down there.' "[3]

Bond's observations were echoed more bitterly by other SNCC staffers, especially those who had always opposed the Summer Project. "I saw white people coming down, telling black people that they should go vote, and all they're going to say, 'Yes, sir,' and 'Yes, ma'am,' and go on and do it. And when they leave, you have destroyed all of that grassroots organizing that was being set forth," Willie Peacock, a native Mississippian and one of the first SNCC field secretaries, recalled. Even Bob Moses, who had worked harder than anyone for an interracial Summer Project, acknowledged by the time the summer ended that the angry feelings Bond and Peacock described had grown worse. "There are very deep tensions," Moses observed. "In some people. In some situations. That is, you can have it. Talk it out. And the deep things come welling out like poison and they spew out over everybody."[4]

During July and August the Summer Project staff and volunteers made sure the tension between them did not, save on rare occasions, reach a point where it interfered with the operation of a project. But in the wake of the Democratic National Convention it was as if the slate had been wiped clean and the restraints of the summer no longer applied. Personal hurts and the organizational problems caused by the Summer Project now assumed a new dimension, clouding all that had been achieved. Within SNCC's ranks the idea of building a civil rights movement in Mississippi that depended on an alliance with Northern whites rapidly became a more bitter issue than ever. "Now we were at loose ends," SNCC's Mary King recalled in her civil rights memoir *Freedom Song*. "We did not yet comprehend that we had dealt a crippling blow to the violence in Mississippi."[5]

For the exhausted Summer Project staff, the fraying of the bonds that once held the project together added a new burden. When in September the staff was invited to travel to Africa, eleven of them—including Fannie Lou Hamer, Julian Bond, Bob Moses, and James Forman—eagerly seized the chance. The trip, which was arranged by singer Harry Belafonte and stemmed from his contacts with the government of President Sékou Touré of Guinea, seemed like a perfect remedy for the strains of the past months. But instead of providing an escape for the SNCC staffers, the trip fueled their frustrations about the alliances they had forged in the course of the summer.[6]

Most striking to the SNCC delegation was that Guinea was an independent nation governed from top to bottom by blacks. That Guinea had also evolved into a one-party state strictly controlled by Sékou Touré made no difference. "I went to Africa in 1964, and I learned that I didn't have anything to be ashamed of from being black," Fannie Lou Hamer wrote. "I saw black people flying the airplanes, driving the buses, sitting behind the big desks in the banks, and just doing everything that I was used to seeing white people do."[7]

James Forman found himself "at home" in a way that he had never felt before. "We belonged here. This was our home. In the United States, we were strangers in a foreign land," he wrote. "My political and historical convictions about the importance of Africa to black people in the United States had become a living experience. My mind was full of ideas and enthusiasm for formalizing and expanding this first link between SNCC, a base of black resistance in the United States, and the African struggle for total independence." Above all, the Guinea trip made it clear to the SNCC delegation that it had not been mistaken in its estimate of the Johnson administration's racial hypocrisy. In Africa the United States government's use of race as a way of making America appealing to Africans was impossible to miss. A shocked Julian Bond noted that there was no mistaking "the kind of deceit" fostered by American information officers. "There were all these pictures of Negroes doing things, Negro judges, Negro policemen," Bond observed, "and if you didn't know anything about America, like most Africans would not, you would think that these were really common-place things."[8]

Meanwhile, in America SNCC now found itself under new attack from the very people who had urged the Freedom Democratic party to accept the president's compromise offer at Atlantic City. At a September 18 meeting at the New York offices of the National Council of Churches, SNCC representatives Courtland Cox and Mendy Samstein were forced to confront not only an angry Joseph Rauh and a bitter former ally, Allard Lowenstein, but hostile representatives from the NAACP and Martin Luther King's Southern Christian Leadership Conference. Believing that the Summer Project had, in the words of SCLC's Andrew Young, the future mayor of Atlanta, "ushered us into a new phase of the civil rights struggle," SNCC's critics now wanted a much bigger say in how decisions were made in Mississippi. To them it was anathema that, as in the case of the MFDP, local people were making decisions that could have national impact.[9]

Within SNCC there was now a growing fear of losing control over the movement it had begun in Mississippi and expanded into a Summer Project. As James Forman put it, "As that meeting at the National Council of Churches made clear, our adversaries were just waiting and hoping for the chance to neutralize or destroy SNCC so that they could manipulate the movement in Mississippi as they wished. If we did not expand our power base there, all kinds of vultures would be waiting to descend on the vacuum." At its October staff meeting SNCC made its first collective attempt to deal with the fact that, as Forman observed, it "was not prepared—structurally, ideologically, or psychologically—to deal with the kinds of enemies we encountered at the Democratic National Convention and afterward." The meeting did not yield the results Forman hoped for. Indeed, it complicated the picture in Mississippi by adding eighty-five new people—most of them summer volunteers—to the SNCC staff. Nonetheless, as the October meeting ended, another meeting was planned that would involve a "total re-examination" of SNCC. In order to guarantee that the new meeting—a week-long gathering scheduled for November 1964 at the Gulfside Church in Waveland, Mississippi—stayed on course, the staff was asked to submit papers in advance, and a special committee was formed to read the papers and set an agenda.[10]

For a SNCC that had traditionally made decisions by consensus, the formalism of Waveland was unprecedented. But as the meeting began, despite the thirty-seven papers submitted for discussion, prospects for resolving SNCC's problems seemed little better than they had been in October. Mississippi-born field secretary Dorie Ladner echoed the feelings of many SNCC veterans when she observed, "The largeness of SNCC is now terrifying."[11] Despite the diversity of the Waveland papers, it soon became apparent that the doubts raised by events at the Democratic convention had taken a deep hold. Waveland would not, like Greenville, lead to a new SNCC project, nor would it produce the kind of organizational reform that James Forman wanted. But reflected in a series of crucial Waveland papers was a skepticism toward black-white alliances and a turning away from outsiders that foreshadowed SNCC's future.

A year earlier at Greenville one of the key defenses of black-white alliances was the example they set. "If we're trying to break down this barrier of segregation, we can't segregate ourselves," Fannie Lou Hamer had warned. Now such alliances were to be judged not by ideals but by the concrete benefits they brought to SNCC. In a paper entitled, "What Is the Importance of Racial Considerations Among the Staff?" Silas Norman, Jr., director of SNCC's operations in Alabama, summed up the new mood, declaring, "I do not know that I am willing to work in an integrated project simply to prove a point."[12]

In Norman's view it was not enough to say that "whites and blacks should be used according to the functions which they best serve." SNCC had to realize that its naiveté about the benefits of white alliances posed a danger. Norman's argument emphasized how often black-white alliances had impeded SNCC's organizing. "It is apparent that whites bring wider publicity and thus wider support," Norman wrote. "Yet it is also apparent that integrated groups in segregated areas are 'spotlights' and that certain groupings, i.e., white women and black men, are a declaration of war." Even in safe areas, Norman insisted, the presence of white workers created a problem for SNCC. Whites put SNCC's black field secretaries in a position where their closeness with the black community was undermined. "There is," Norman declared, "a sort of ethnic relationship among the staff and the community," and "this relationship cannot be entered into by whites."[13]

Norman's euphemism for black solidarity—"a sort of ethnic relationship"—was a sign of how difficult it was for many in SNCC to voice criticism of whites while still meeting with them. As paper after paper showed, SNCC's staffers shared a concern that their organizing had been hampered by deference to white middle-class values. "New habits must be learned," Maria Varela, head of SNCC's literacy project, warned. "We still have the habits that come from a system of values that almost all of us have had—that is that educated, better-off people naturally dominate under-educated, less well-off people."[14]

A year earlier, when complaints were raised about the role of whites in SNCC, advocates of the Summer Project insisted that time and closer contact would improve race relations. Now, at Waveland, a different view of the future prevailed. As SNCC field secretary Charles Sherrod observed in his paper, whites were under increasing pressure to abandon SNCC or persuade it to modify its aims. In the past, Sherrod noted, SNCC had made inroads by "using the symbols of what hundreds of bodies mean together" and by an appeal to "the white man's guilt." That era was now at an end, he warned. "There is a 'backlash' of the white man's conscience. There is a point at which the whites in our country are saying outside the NO's that have been present inside of them all the time."[15]

Sherrod's solution to what he saw as the coming bad times was for SNCC to remember on whom and on what it was based. In his account of the MFDP's refusal to accept the Atlantic City compromise, Sherrod had written, "We had not bowed to the 'massa.'" At Waveland he extended that view further. "A man may be so ignorant [that he can't] make a pair of shoes, but not so ignorant that he doesn't know when a pair of shoes pinches him or that the roof leaks or that white folks have power over [the fact] that his belly is empty," Sherrod declared. "We must demand that the new society for which we strive be based on the wisdom of the pinched toe and the empty belly." How many whites, especially those middle-class college students who had come to Mississippi during the summer, had such wisdom? In the context of Waveland, the answer to Sherrod's question was self-evident. Neither he nor the other advocates of a new reality needed to spell out their feelings.[16]

A year earlier at Greenville, when it looked like there might not be a Summer Project, Bob Moses had put his reputation on the line and argued for a project that made extensive use of white volunteers. But at Waveland Moses took no such stance. "We are on a boat in the middle of the ocean. It has to be rebuilt in order to stay afloat. It also has to stay afloat in order to be rebuilt," he observed in his paper. It was a dilemma for which Moses saw no clear solution. Throughout Waveland he remained in the background, starting along a road that would lead him to resign as director of COFO by the end of the year and slowly to withdraw from SNCC leadership.[17]

The way was now open for SNCC to pursue a course very different from that of the summer of 1964. In December 1964 the FBI arrested twenty-one men, including the sheriff and deputy sheriff of Neshoba County, for the murders of Schwerner, Chaney, and Goodman, but the arrests drew little reaction from SNCC. The depth of feelings expressed at Waveland about the role of whites in the civil rights movement was evident just three months later at SNCC's February staff meeting in Atlanta. At a session that began with Mississippi field secretary Jesse Morris proposing that all members of SNCC's executive committee must be black, come from the South, and have no more than a high school education, SNCC chairman John Lewis delivered a speech which outlined the thinking of the post-1964 SNCC.[18]

Lewis, who had stayed on in Africa after most of the SNCC delegation returned home, began by comparing the situation of blacks in America and Africa. "I am convinced more than ever before that the social, economic, and political destiny of the black people of America is inseparable from that of our black brothers of Africa. It matters not whether it is in Angola, Mozambique, Southwest Africa, or Mississippi, Alabama, Georgia, and Harlem, U.S.A. The struggle is one of the same," Lewis declared. "It is a struggle against

a vicious and evil system that is controlled and kept in order
for and by a few white men throughout the world." Lewis did
not deny that in America there were many poor whites who
were "victims of the evils of the economic and political
system." His point was rather that white suffering was not
collectively the same as black suffering. "Black people feel
these evils more for we are not only economically exploited
and politically denied but we are also dehumanized by the
vicious system of segregation and racial discrimination."[19]

From this difference, Lewis argued, it followed that
SNCC had a special task. SNCC had to make "the liberation
of black people" its primary concern, and it had to do so with
the knowledge that such liberation required "revolutionary"
change. "Too many of us are too busy telling white people
that we are now ready to be integrated into their society,"
Lewis warned. "We must dig deep into the black centers of
power throughout this nation not just for financial reasons but
as a base of political support. I am convinced that this
country is a racist country. The majority of the population is
white, and most whites still hold a master-slave mentality."[20]

The momentous implications of Lewis's argument were
not lost on his SNCC audience. While he was not advocating
that SNCC spurn all white help, he was pointing out how
uncertain and unreliable most of it—along with most middle-
class help in general—was bound to be. "I think past history
will testify to the fact that white liberals and the so-called
affluent Negro leaders will not support all our demands," Lewis
declared. "They will be forced to support some of them in
order to maintain an image of themselves as liberal. But we
must also recognize that their material comforts and congen-
ial relations with the establishment are much more important
to them than their concern for an oppressed people. And they
will sell us down the river for the hundredth time in order to
protect themselves. We all saw this in Atlantic City." Under
these circumstances, Lewis concluded, there was only one

alternative. "If the movement and SNCC are going to be effective in attempting to liberate the black masses, the civil rights movement must be black-controlled, dominated, and led."[21]

The kind of civil rights movement symbolized by the Summer Project was over. Lewis's speech, despite his own willingness to work with whites, was the epitaph for the hopes that Bob Moses had voiced at Greenville when he insisted, "The one thing we can do for the country that no one else can do is to be above the race issue." It was more than a year before whites were officially expelled from SNCC, but the groundwork had been laid for a SNCC that believed, "If we are to proceed toward true liberation, we must cut ourselves off from white people. We must form our own institutions, credit unions, co-ops, political parties, write our own histories." In 1966, when after a bitter election struggle Stokely Carmichael succeeded John Lewis as SNCC chairman, SNCC's commitment to black power soon became unmistakable to the nation. But the Stokely Carmichael who captured newspaper headlines by leading black-power rallies during the 1966 Meredith March in Mississippi was—his personal flamboyance notwithstanding—no SNCC renegade. He stood for a culmination of feelings which were already apparent by Waveland. Nothing John Lewis had said a few months after Waveland needed to be fundamentally changed in order to accommodate Carmichael's black-power assertion, "Only black people can convey the revolutionary idea— and it is a revolutionary idea—that black people are able to do things themselves. Only they can help create in the community an aroused and continuing black consciousness that will provide the basis for political strength." The path to black power had been cleared by the door that closed on the Freedom Democratic party in Atlantic City.[22]

●　　●　　●

SNCC's growing distance from the Summer Project volunteers was heightened by the volunteers' growing distance from Mississippi. As the fall of 1964 began, volunteers too found themselves rethinking the summer. As Pam Parker wrote to her parents, "No one can go through an experience such as Mississippi without coming out changed. I do not believe that many of those who spent their summer in Mississippi will be able to go back to their old way of living." Bob Moses would later speculate that if the Summer Project had concluded with a carefully planned debriefing of the volunteers (one that both thanked them for their contribution and sent them home), many of the internal problems that arose after Atlantic City might have been avoided. But by the end of August the project staff was too exhausted to worry about the volunteers. The latter would have to deal by themselves with the problems posed by the Summer Project.[23]

For volunteers who remained in Mississippi, it quickly became clear that although they had been asked to stay their presence was now a source of heightened tension. In December SNCC field secretary Hunter Morey described the tensions between whites and blacks as a threat to everything the Summer Project had achieved. "We are faced with both the greatest dangers and the greatest opportunities of our short life. After finally making Mississippi a pressing national issue, COFO is torn with internal disorganization of almost fatal proportions if not quickly remedied," Morey wrote. "White workers are often subject to severe racial abuse and even violence from Negro workers. . . . Negro workers are frequently played-up-to and looked-down-on by white workers." But even without such confrontations, the volunteers who remained in Mississippi could not fail to see that they had become a major problem for SNCC. The opposition to adding eighty-five volunteers to the SNCC staff had been led by James Forman and Ruby Doris Robinson, two of the organization's most respected figures, and by Waveland it was apparent from the papers submitted that SNCC was spending almost as much time thinking about the Northern whites in its midst as the Southern whites it had been organized to fight.[24]

The volunteers who returned North were spared such confrontations, but the problems they experienced from afar were nonetheless painful. In Mississippi the volunteers had fought a war that in its daily skirmishes and absence of a front line was strikingly like the war in Vietnam; and on returning home—alone or in car pools of two and three—they felt more isolated than ever. Years later Pam Parker, in a workshop on post-traumatic stress disorder, found the anxieties of Vietnam veterans very much like those she experienced after Mississippi. But in 1964 volunteers like Parker did not have workshops, let alone a terminology, for dealing with their reactions to Mississippi. There were no victory parades waiting for them and few people who understood what they had gone through. As one volunteer wrote to friends still in Mississippi, "You can't think or remember or go back because *in the North Mississippi doesn't exist.*"[25]

The first problem faced by the volunteers was picking up routines they had left behind. As the summer wound to a close, the volunteers had imagined returning home. Hundreds of miles away the familiar seemed wonderful. "I am tired," a Holly Springs volunteer complained in a typical end-of-the-summer letter. "I want to go very much to a movie, or to watch TV even. I want to be in Berkeley and do stupid things and don't look behind me in the rearview mirror." Once the volunteers returned North, they found, however, that these longed-for routines quickly lost their appeal. The familiar was now a dreary middle-class burden, carrying with it the kinds of questions Sally Belfrage had asked herself with the end of the Summer Project in sight: "How can I leave? How can I leave people I love so much? What made me think I could accomplish anything in this length of time?"[26]

In Mississippi the volunteers' lives had been speeded up. Just surviving was an achievement. Now college and home seemed tame. "There is a certainty, when you are working in Mississippi, that it is important for you to be alive and to be alive just doing what you are doing," a Meridian volunteer observed. "Twenty-four hours a day your life is caught up with a very important purpose," Nancy Jervis recalled. "What else has meaning like that?" In the fall's *Harvard Crimson* registration issue, which was devoted to Mississippi, Peter Cummings used similar language to describe his experiences. "Mississippi is at once the worst and the best. It is a nightmare of fear and tension, quite literally a police state. Yet it also has the most thoroughly organized and strongest freedom movement in the nation," Cummings wrote. "The freedom worker lives in the nightmare and the dream world every day." There was, the volunteers finally realized, no way to categorize their experiences. The real difference was before and after. "I don't think anybody who claims to have seen the Virgin Mary had as intense a religious experience as I did in Mississippi," Lester Galt remembered. "This was easily the pivotal event of my life."[27]

For volunteer after volunteer, the loss of such excitement and purpose was a letdown. Complaints of depression were frequent. In suburban New Jersey Nancy Schieffelin imagined herself doing violence to neighbors who showed no concern with what was going on in Mississippi. "I had come back in a rage and experienced fantasies of blowing up people's houses in Short Hills. That's how mad I was," she recalled. At the University of Chicago Law School Len Edwards found that just controlling his emotions was a task. "We only get a few chances in this short life of ours to play a role in history and do something we believe in," he later observed. "When the summer was over, there wasn't that common goal any longer."[28]

The volunteers who returned to colleges that had sent groups of students south had the solace of one another's company, but time and again it was hard for the volunteers to imagine being in school. "I really don't want to go back to New Haven. It seems a crime to turn these kids back to a school system that won't even admit its own deficiencies," Gene Nelson wrote to his parents from Holly Springs. "A year at Swarthmore now will make me hate education and get me a diploma," Gretchen Schwartz wrote to her parents from Ruleville. "I'd be miserable and waste a great deal of your money at Swarthmore. I must stay now."[29]

After Mississippi the volunteers found that other people their own age seemed tremendously naive. "In St. Paul, I talked to twenty college students, their bland white faces in a circle around me," a volunteer from Minnesota wrote. "We drank coffee from little china teacups, drawn from silver coffee urns, all elegance and tastefulness. My backdrop was a heavy, large fireplace. Muzak floated through the air, homogenized. I was passionate. And later I thought, how comic and grim, how can the Mississippi Delta exist for these kids except as a fairy tale, because getting into the one reality means canceling out the other reality." At Brown, Nancy Schieffelin realized that there was now no way for her to make sense of college social life. "When I got back on campus people were going about their lives, and it had nothing to do with what I had been going through," she recalled. "People were concerned about what they were going to wear on their dates, and that seemed so irrelevant in my mind."[30]

But it was not only their fellow students who struck the volunteers as naive. After a summer in Mississippi, the volunteers also had a sense of becoming older than their parents, of dealing with realities their parents' generation had chosen to ignore. "The old comforts were thrown into question," Nancy Schieffelin recalled. "I realized that my parents couldn't understand me. They were no longer a source of safety." Schieffelin was not unique in feeling she had gone through experiences her parents could not comprehend. Arguing that she should be allowed to drop out of college for a year, an angry Ellen Lake wrote to her parents, "Maturity does not develop from facing a familiar routine from year to year. Maturity comes from having to face new situations, from making new decisions, from coming to terms with a new world."[31]

Especially difficult for the returning volunteers were the comforts of home life. "Here was a family I totally loved and whose values I felt led me to the Summer Project, and there was this terrible rift. It was the first time there had ever been a split between me and my folks," Heather Tobis remembered. "At the end of the summer I felt I couldn't find words. It was two cultures. I was in a place where there were dirt roads and no indoor plumbing and kids got worms through their feet because they didn't have shoes, and you go from there to a society where people have two cars and want to know which college of your choice you're going to." In Pam Parker's case the rift with her parents began when she realized just how much she had taken for granted her family's style of living. "We were not rich, but four families could live well in Mississippi on what my family lived on. It was something I couldn't cope with," she remembered thinking. An end-of-the-summer vacation only made things worse. What she had returned to from Mississippi—"the deadness of white middle-class America"—now seemed more threatening than ever. "I just freaked out," Parker recalled. As a favor to her father, she returned to Carlton College to finish her senior year, but the estrangement between her and her parents continued for years. Later, after reading an article by Carolyn Goodman, the mother of Andrew Goodman, Parker's mother wrote to Mrs. Goodman, "You lost your son, but I've lost my daughter."[32]

As a way of retaining their connection with Mississippi, many of the volunteers helped to raise funds and publicize the work of the Summer Project. But more often than not, such work failed to relieve the volunteers' sense of alienation. When they tried to talk seriously about Mississippi, the volunteers found that frequently people didn't really want to hear them. "People want a nice-handy three-word phrase to be able to repeat to neighbors," a Westchester volunteer wrote. "They ask me a question, then start talking before I can answer." In North Dakota, Lester Galt ran into a similar situation. "I expected other North Dakotans to respond as I had responded. When they didn't, I would get frustrated," he remembered. "There was a rough four or five months there when I was so on fire and needed everybody to see it the way I saw it. I would just get angry when they didn't."[33]

After a summer in Mississippi a risk-free life was a guilty life for most volunteers. "All during the summer there was the sense that you can always leave and go back to safety, but these folks have to stay and live with the situation. That always concerned me a lot. It was part of why I wanted to stay," Ruleville volunteer Linda Davis remembered thinking. A Columbus volunteer wrote: "Reasons for not staying are easy to amass, but everyone, including the rationalizer himself, suspects these reasons. We can't feel as though things are solid enough to keep going without us." Thinking first of one's own educational future now seemed like self-indulgence. "The people with whom I have been working have come to know and to trust me. I cannot let them down by leaving just when violence and terror show signs of increasing," Marshall Ganz wrote to the administrative board of Harvard in his petition for a leave of absence. "It would be impossible for me to exchange the reality and importance of our work in Mississippi for a book."[34]

The safety of life in the North made some volunteers feel nothing short of deceitful. "When I came back to

California, one of the things I used to say was, 'I'm home. I'm safe.' But the people I've left behind are not safe. Part of me felt like a deserter," Margaret Aley remembered. In Mississippi the volunteers—women as well as men—had taken pride in thinking of themselves as soldiers in a civil rights war. Back home they now used that terminology to disparage their situation. What kind of bravery were they showing, they asked themselves, if they left the battlefield before the war was over? "The summer is only the briefest beginning of this experience—both for myself and for the Negroes of Mississippi," Ellen Lake wrote to her parents. "So much of it will seem pointless if it ends now, or if it is taken up again in two years. A war cannot be fought and won if the soldiers take twelve-month leaves after every skirmish." Volunteer Dennis Flannigan was even harsher on himself, looking on his situation from the perspective of a survivor who hadn't taken enough chances with his own life. "There was a shame of not being Bob Moses, of not being there," he remembered. "The job wasn't over. It was like a war you left. Any soldier going home knows that if the war isn't over he's leaving buddies to die."[35]

But the volunteers would make no collective return to the war they had left behind. Over the course of the 1960s the Berkeley Free Speech Movement, the Vietnam antiwar movement, the women's movement, the United Farm Workers' struggles would all be influenced by the volunteers; but the passage of time would also make it clear to them that in the eyes of SNCC they were no longer welcome in Mississippi. It was their final and most painful burden to bear—one that brought the volunteers full circle from the time when they were told, "Mississippi will not change until there are white people working with Negroes to change it."[36]

"I was hurt by the hatred that blacks were beginning to express toward people like me who had worked for years to achieve integration," Paul Cowan later wrote in his *The*

Making of an Un-American. "I could accept the cultural explanation for their efforts to rid their organizations of whites, but no rational arguments really healed the pain of the personal attacks." For volunteers like Cowan there were no good alternatives. If they spoke out in protest, they gave comfort to the most reactionary forces in Mississippi. If they remained silent, they did violence to their own deepest feelings.[37]

The irony is that as the volunteers and Summer Project staff moved farther apart, recognition of what they had achieved together was growing. In his December 1964 speech accepting the Nobel Peace Prize, Martin Luther King could count on his worldwide audience understanding him when he declared, "I am mindful that only yesterday in Philadelphia, Mississippi, young people seeking to secure the right to vote were brutalized and murdered."[38] Thanks to the Summer Project, Mississippi had come to be a place of hope as well as a symbol for what the Southern way of life meant in America if you weren't white.

11

Mississippi Revisited

If any event sums up how deep racial hatred went in the Mississippi of 1964, it is the funeral of James Chaney. His parents and those of Michael Schwerner had hoped that their murdered sons might be buried next to each other. But in the Mississippi of 1964, segregation applied as much in death as in life. No white undertaker would transport Michael Schwerner's body to a black cemetery, and the black undertaker handling James Chaney's funeral feared that he would lose his license if he handled a white body. In the end both families bowed to reality. The Schwerners arranged to have their son's body flown back to New York. James Chaney was buried August 7 at a new black cemetery atop Mount Barton, less than an hour after his body was returned to Meridian from the University of Mississippi Medical Center in Jackson.[1]

That same night, at a memorial service at the First Union Baptist Church in Meridian, Dave Dennis, assistant director of the Summer Project and the CORE official who had approved the decision to send Schwerner, Chaney, and Goodman into the county where they met their deaths, delivered a bitter eulogy. "As I stand here I not only blame the people who pulled the trigger or did the beating or dug the hole with the shovel. I blame the people in Washington, D.C., and on down in the state of Mississippi for what happened just as much as I blame those who pulled the trigger," Dennis declared. "I'm sick and tired of going to the funerals of black men who have been murdered by white men. I've got vengeance in my heart tonight, and I ask you to feel angry with me. I'k and tired, and I ask you to be sick and tired with me."[2]

On June 21, 1989, twenty-five years to the day that Michael Schwerner, James Chaney, and Andrew Goodman were murdered, a very different mood prevailed among the crowd gathered for the memorial service at the Mount Zion Methodist Church in Philadelphia, Mississippi. The question on everyone's mind was what the governor and the secretary of state would have to say. Much had changed in Philadelphia and Neshoba County since 1964. The public schools had been integrated. The Mount Zion Church had been rebuilt after it was burned to the ground. Seven of the men responsible for the murders of Schwerner, Chaney, and Goodman had gone to prison. But frank talk about the murders still made people in Mississippi uneasy, especially in this part of the state.[3]

No one understood this feeling better than Mississippi Secretary of State Dick Molpus. He had grown up in Philadelphia before going on to college at Ole Miss and becoming one of "the boys of spring" who helped William Winter, a reform governor, pass Mississippi's Education Reform Act, making school compulsory for the first time in the state's history. A popular secretary of state, Molpus had been told by his advisers that becoming actively involved in the memorial service for Schwerner, Chaney, and Goodman was a risk; but he had found the commemoration an event he could not bypass. "I thought that my community had been looking for the last twenty-five years for a way to address this," he said later. "What we had here was the opportunity for a cathartic experience."[4]

As Molpus began the short speech that had taken him three weeks to write, it became clear that he would hold back nothing. No sooner had he completed his welcoming remarks than he announced that he had a special word for the families of the three men. "We deeply regret what happened here twenty-five years ago. We wish we could undo it. We are profoundly sorry that they are gone," he declared. "We wish we could bring them back. Every decent person in Philadelphia and Neshoba County and Mississippi feels that way." The applause began, then almost as quickly died down. It was too much like clapping in the middle of a minister's sermon. Molpus went on. "Today we pay tribute to those who died. We acknowledge that dark corner in our past." From this point on, it did not matter what else Molpus said. He had done what no one was sure any elected white official in Mississippi would ever do: he had apologized for the racial violence that his state had once condoned.[5]

Molpus was not the only official to speak for Mississippi and to apologize for its past that day. Ray Mabus, Jr., the new Mississippi governor and, like Molpus, a former member of the Winter administration, was equally determined to deal with the dark corner of 1964. Mabus had taken office in 1988, winning the black vote 9 to 1 and promising "basic, drastic, change." In his speech it was clear that he too saw 1964 as a turning point. "The tragedy of these three young men and our tragedy have been analyzed, scrutinized, and debated. Was their sacrifice worth it? Did they make a difference? All of us know the answer. Look around," the governor urged. A memorial like this was not, he insisted, just a testimony to "three brave young men who will remain forever young." It was an historic occasion in its own right, an acknowledgment of the "many times unseen and unheard of bravery of thousands of others who struggled and who suffered and who, in some cases, died for the same idea, the same dream."[6]

In the summer of 1964 Dick Molpus was fourteen. Most of his days were spent working, as he always did during vacations, in the family lumber business his grandfather began in Philadelphia in 1905. Molpus remembers vividly the murders of the civil rights workers and the shock of seeing Ku Klux Klansmen light a giant cross on the grounds of the Neshoba County courthouse. He also remembers his father's response to the men who came to his office with a list of black employees who had been seen going to NAACP meetings. His father had not done as he was asked and fired the employees. Instead he had shown his visitors to the door and hired two local men he could trust to watch over his lumberyard at night.[7]

Ray Mabus was fifteen that summer, living forty-five miles away from Philadelphia in the small town of Ackerman, where his family had first settled in 1830. None of the Philadelphia violence ever reached the town where Mabus lived, but like Molpus he remembers the murders, and he remembers his father sitting him down and talking about the rule of law. His father had given him a similar talk two years earlier when rioting had broken out upon James Meredith entering Ole Miss, and for Mabus the two events came to symbolize what segregation meant in the Mississippi he knew. That fall, in a high school where the straw election went 234 to 1 for Goldwater, Mabus was the one student in assembly to speak up for the need to elect Lyndon Johnson. Among his friends he would be remembered for holding up a can of Johnson's wax and offering to remove the Goldwater bumper sticker from anyone's car.[8]

Teenagers like Dick Molpus and Ray Mabus were not the kinds of whites whom Summer Project workers got close to in 1964. They were too young, and for someone who did not know their families, they were impossible to pick out from the kids who meant trouble. Who had time to hope that one of them might turn out to be a Huck Finn? Who could know that they would help constitute the first generation of white Mississippi politicians to take office without blood on their hands?

Three decades after the Summer Project, it is not only men like Molpus and Mabus who have shown they can get elected in Mississippi. As of January 1989 Mississippi had 646 black elected officials, more than any other state. They included black congressman Mike Espy, a black state supreme court justice, twenty-two black state legislators, almost seventy black county supervisors, more than twenty-five black mayors, and 282 black city council members. These days, as Espy points out, "If you're going to get elected to anything in Mississippi, you have to pay attention to and court the black vote." But there is also part of Mississippi that has not changed dramatically since 1964. Drive down Lynch Street in the black section of Jackson and stop at 1017, where the Summer Project had its offices in 1964, and what you see is a shabby, boarded-up building that was last known as Mary's Lounge. Lynch Street's reminders of the past are the unpainted shotgun houses that line both sides of the street and look as if a strong wind would knock them off their crumbling foundations. To be black in Mississippi is still to be poor and to have trouble finding a good job. In 1990 when the predominantly black work force at the Delta Pride Catfish plant in Indianola went out on strike, it was because the wages they were averaging for full-time work came to $4.05 an hour, or less than $8,500 per year. What had prompted the Delta Pride workers to take such low-paying jobs was a black unemployment rate in Mississippi of 13.2 percent, more than double that of whites.[9]

A Third Reconstruction—historian C. Vann Woodward's term for an era in which the economic life of black America would be transformed in a way that parallels the changes brought about by the civil rights movement—never followed the Summer Project in Mississippi or anywhere else in the nation. There is a difference, however, in calling for a Third Reconstruction today, when the median income of black families is 59.4 percent that of whites—a lower figure than in 1970—and in the 1960s when there was a clear belief that with the civil rights movement plus the Great Society programs of Lyndon Johnson it would be only a matter of time until America was economically integrated.[10]

In the 1960s the idea of a permanent black underclass or of third- and fourth-generation welfare families seemed, the Moynihan Report of 1965 notwithstanding, unthinkable to most people, especially liberals. Remedies for poverty even produced a shared language. In 1967, the year C. Vann Woodward asked, "How long before the country will be prepared to face up to a Third Reconstruction?" affirmative action did not pit whites against blacks or threaten to make race a credential. In that year the meaning of affirmative action was spelled out clearly in Lyndon Johnson's Executive Order 11375: "The contractor will not discriminate against any employee or applicant because of race, color, religion, sex, or national origin. The contractor will take affirmative

action to ensure that employees are treated during employment without regard to their race, color, religion, sex, or
national origin."[11]

Today we live in a racially pessimistic America, shaped
by more than a decade of constant attacks on the social
programs of the 1960s. When George Bush ran for the
Senate in Texas in 1964 and opposed the civil rights bill of
1964, he made himself an easy political target. Bush lost to
Democratic Senator Ralph Yarborough by a 56 to 44 margin
and won only 3 percent of the black vote. But three decades
later, when George Bush labeled the bill that would finally
become the Civil Rights Act of 1991 a "quota bill," it was a
very different story. Bush was not only speaking as the
president, he was using a code word that he could count on
to fuel the feelings of racial resentment that made a television
commercial about Willie Horton and the Massachusetts prison
furlough system so effective in his 1988 campaign.[12]

These days such feelings of racial resentment are not
confined to politics. Among a growing number of once-
liberal historians with, as they put it, "second thoughts"
about the 1960s, the current orthodoxy is that the SNCC
"militants" of 1964 are the source of our present racial
schisms. According to the second-thoughts scenario, the
militants' angry rejection of the compromise offered to the
Mississippi Freedom Democratic party at the Democratic
National Convention of 1964 was the event that started us
down the path toward the black nationalism and revolutionary
posturing of the late 1960s, and finally to the racial polari-
zation we now face.[13]

In terms of those it blames and those it exonerates, it is
a scenario that lends itself to the kind of racial scapegoating
that was part of 1990s culture even before the Rodney King
trial and Los Angeles riots of 1992 made everything worse.
More to the point, it is a scenario that is historically inaccur-
ate. It telescopes too many events. What really happened in

1964 is both more complex and more difficult to undo. The second-thoughts historians are correct in one respect, however: the racial frustrations of 1964 did mark the beginning of the end of an effective black-white coalition politics in America. The Democratic party's rejection of the claims of the Mississippi Freedom Democratic party fatally undermined the arguments that had been advanced within the Summer Project for alliances with liberal whites; and when those arguments were undermined, a power vacuum was created in SNCC that opened the door for it to depart from the course it had followed with such difficulty in the summer of 1964. The views of those who had opposed the Summer Project and no longer wanted to work with whites now had new authority.[14]

By the fall of 1964 SNCC was on its way to becoming an organization that would make it impossible even for longtime white field secretaries like Bob Zellner to remain a part of it. A Stokely Carmichael talking about black power in 1966 could use language that sounded very much like what John Lewis had employed after his 1964 trip to Africa, when he called for a SNCC that would be "black controlled, dominated, and led." But in Stokely Carmichael's hands black power meant more than black empowerment. It also meant dealing with whites as "whitey" and "honky" and establishing a SNCC in which a cult of personality—one that identified the organization with a single individual—replaced the style of self-effacing leadership epitomized by Bob Moses.[15]

In the SNCC of Stokely Carmichael and his successor, H. Rap Brown, racial hatred became fashionable. In a 1964 interview Bob Moses, citing the French philosopher Albert Camus, had worried out loud about how easy it was in any social revolution for victims and executioners to change places. By the late 1960s writer Julius Lester, who had joined SNCC's staff shortly after Carmichael became chairman, reflected the new mood in SNCC by turning Bob Moses's fears upside down. "It is clearly written that the victim must become the executioner," Lester proclaimed in his widely read 1968 book *Look Out Whitey! Black Power's Gon' Get Your Mama!* A year earlier a leaflet by SNCC's Chicago staff had been even more candid, declaring, "We must fill ourselves with hate for all things white."[16]

"We made a serious mistake when the movement turned against its first principle: integration. The seeds that were planted twenty years ago have borne very bitter fruit," John Lewis observed shortly before the 1989 memorial service for Schwerner, Chaney, and Goodman. These days Lewis is not alone in his belief that when the civil rights movement of the 1960s broke apart along racial lines it opened a schism which gave new legitimacy to its enemies. Three decades later there is, however, no going back and undoing the past.[17]

There is no way now to argue for a smaller Summer Project that would put less strain on SNCC and allow for more control at the grassroots. There is no way now for Bob Moses to hold, as he would later imagine, an end-of-the-summer debriefing that thanked the volunteers, then sent all of them home, leaving SNCC once again on its own in Mississippi. And there is no way now to persuade the SNCC staff that, bitter as it was, the Freedom Democratic party compromise in Atlantic City had a positive side: beginning in 1968 no Democratic convention delegation, including Mississippi's, would ever again be segregated.[18]

But although we cannot like time travelers go back to 1964 and reclaim the opportunities we had then for changing history, we need not abandon the legacy of the Summer Project. That legacy is present today not just on occasions like the Schwerner, Chaney, and Goodman memorial service. It exists at the local level in a city like Jackson, Mississippi, where, after a long history of white flight, white parents are making a deliberate effort to integrate the city school system. It exists at the national level where a sociologist like the University of Chicago's William Julius Wilson strives to replace a divisive politics of affirmative action with race-neutral programs that allow blacks and whites to work as allies for social welfare legislation.[19]

We make a grave error if we think that the legacy of the Mississippi Summer Project demands of us the kind of political nostalgia that amounts to imitation. At the heart of the Summer Project was a black-white coalition which, along with defying history, defied assimilationist fears that in such an alliance black values and black leaders would inevitably lose their power. It was the spectacle of a civil rights army prepared to be killed but not to kill that first drew the nation's attention to Mississippi. But as the Summer Project wore on, became in effect our 1960s good war, it was the Summer Project coalition itself and the belief it embodied that common ground could be found among blacks and whites that gave the nation hope. What a history of the Summer Project allows us to see three decades later is how vital the example of such a coalition remains; how much must happen before it can come into being; how easily the sensibility it personifies is lost.

A Note on Sources

I have been greatly aided by the willingness of those who were part of the Summer Project to speak with me. In my text I have used the names they used in 1964, but my notes and interview list reflect the name changes adopted by many of them for personal or political reasons.

INTERVIEW LIST

Margaret Aley / Margaret Aley Chavez
Lisa Anderson / Lisa Anderson Todd
Sam Block
Charlie Cobb
MacArthur Cotton
Courtland Cox
Linda Davis
John Doar
Len Edwards
Dennis Flannigan
James Forman
Lester Galt
Marshall Ganz
Victoria Gray / Victoria Gray Adams
Lawrence Guyot
Casey Hayden / Sandra Carson
Curtis Hayes / Curtis Hayes Muhammad
Jan Hillegas
Sam Howze / Sala Udin
Lewis Hyde
Nancy Jervis
Mary King
Dorie Ladner
John Lewis
Staughton Lynd
Ray Mabus, Jr.

Dick Molpus
Bob Moses
Bill Moyers
Robbie Osman
Pam Parker / Chude Pam Allen
Willie Peacock / Wazir Peacock
Frank Roosevelt
Nancy Schieffelin
Frank Smith
Matt Suarez
Muriel Tillinghast
Heather Tobis / Heather Tobis Booth
Pat Vail
Hollis Watkins
Bob Zellner
Dorothy Zellner

COPIES OF LETTERS AND NOTEBOOKS IN AUTHOR'S POSSESSION

Margaret Aley / Margaret Aley Chavez
Pam Parker / Chude Pam Allen
Stuart Rawlings
Ron de Souza
Greenville Whitman

ABBREVIATIONS USED IN THE NOTES

CRCUT, Civil Rights Collection, University of Tennessee, Knoxville

LBJ, Lyndon B. Johnson Presidential Library, Austin, Texas

MIBURN, Mississippi Burning Files of the FBI obtained from the U.S. Department of Justice under the Freedom of Information Act

MLK, Martin Luther King, Jr., Library and Archives, Atlanta, Georgia

MSRS, Moorland-Spingarn Research Center, Howard University, Washington, D.C.

SI, Smithsonian Institution, Voices of the Civil Rights Movement, National Museum of American History, Washington, D.C.

SHSW, State Historical Society of Wisconsin, Madison

SNCC Papers, Student Nonviolent Coordinating Committee Papers, 1959–1972 (Microfilm Corporation of America)

UCLA, Civil Rights Movement, Special Collections, University Research Library, University of California at Los Angeles

Notes

1. Introduction: Like a Holy Crusade

1. Signed Statement of Horace Doyle Barnette, November, 20, 1964, File JN44-1, Federal Bureau of Investigation, MIBURN. Don Whitehead, *Attack on Terror: The FBI Against the Ku Klux Klan in Mississippi* (New York, 1970), p. 277. Seth Cagin and Philip Dray, *We Are Not Afraid: The Story of Goodman, Schwerner, and Chaney, and the Civil Rights Campaign for Mississippi* (New York, 1988), pp. 278–300.

2. On the number of volunteers in Mississippi, see Doug McAdam, *Freedom Summer* (New York, 1988), p. 7. SNCC Papers: Executive Committee, Memorandum to All SNCC Project Heads, February 24, 1964, A-II-3, Reel 3. Exactly 6.7 percent of eligible black voters were registered in Mississippi in 1964; U.S. Commission on Civil Rights, *Hearings on Civil Rights Held in Jackson, Mississippi* (Washington, D.C., February 16–20, 1965), p. 177.

3. On the number of SNCC staffers on the Summer Project, see Cagin and Dray, *We Are Not Afraid*, p. 219. *Jackson Clarion-Ledger*, June 30, 1964, p. 4.

4. James W. Loewen and Charles Sallis, *Mississippi: Conflict and Change* (New York, 1974), p. 178. Governor Paul Johnson, Jr., quoted in Jesse Kornbluth, "The '64 Civil Rights Murders: The Struggle Continues," *New York Times Magazine*, July 23, 1989, p. 18. McAdam, *Freedom Summer*, pp. 25, 292.

5. John Lewis quoted in James Atwater, "If We Can Crack Mississippi," *Saturday Evening Post*, July 25/August 1, 1964, p. 19. Clayborne Carson, *In Struggle: SNCC and the Black Awakening of the 1980s* (Cambridge, Mass., 1982), p. 58. Carl M. Brauer, *John F. Kennedy and the Second Reconstruction* (New York, 1977), pp. 260, 277–279. Robert Weisbrot, *Freedom Bound: A History of America's Civil Rights Movement* (New York, 1988), pp. 125–127.

6. Thomas Byrne Edsall and Mary D. Edsall, *Chain Reaction: The Impact of Race, Rights, and Taxes on American Politics* (New York, 1991), p. 36.

7. SHSW: Anne Romaine Interview with Bob Moses, Part II, September 5, 1966, p. 18.

8. Milton Viorst, *Fire in the Streets* (New York, 1979), p. 250. Neil R. McMillen, "Black Enfranchisement in Mississippi: Federal Enforcement and

Black Protest in the 1960s," *Journal of Southern History*, XLIII (August 1977), 352.

9. SHSW: Howard Zinn Papers, Notes on Mississippi Staff Meeting, November 1963, p. 28.

10. Volunteer quoted in Sally Belfrage, *Freedom Summer* (New York, 1965), p. 10. Interview with Len Edwards, September 5, 1991.

11. U.S. Commission on Civil Rights, *Hearings on Civil Rights*, p. 157.

12. David Chalmers, "Committed, Proud, and Distrustful: The Mississippi Freedom Volunteers 20 Years Later," *USA Today Magazine*, September 1984, p. 38.

13. Bob Moses quoted in *New Yorker*, April 11, 1964, p. 36.

14. Louis Harris Survey on the Summer Project in *Newsweek*, July 12, 1964, p 24.

15. U.S. Commission on Civil Rights, *Hearings on Civil Rights*, p. 177 U.S. Commission on Civil Rights, *The Voting Rights Act: Ten Years After*, (Washington, D.C., January 1975), pp. 52–53. Pat Watters and Reese Cleghorn, *Climbing Jacob's Ladder* (New York, 1967), p. 247. McMillen, "Black Enfranchisement," pp. 352–372.

16. John Lewis, "Mississippi Freedom Summer—20 Years Later," *Dissent*, Winter 1985, p. 15. Thomas B. Edsall, "Rights Drive Said to Lose Underpinnings," *Washington Post*, March 9, 1991, p. A6.

17. With regard to the second wave, see in particular Carson, *In Struggle;* McAdam, *Freedom Summer;* and Cagin and Dray, *We Are Not Afraid*. On the mood among neoconservatives and liberals, see Peter Collier and David Horowitz, eds., *Second Thoughts About Race in America* (Landham, Md., 1992), and "Opinions Considered: A Talk with Tom Wicker," *New York Times*, January 5, 1992, p. E4.

18. Mary King, *Freedom Song* (New York, 1987), p. 379.

19. Interview with Robbie Osman, August 23, 1991.

2. Burn Jim Crow to the Ground

1. King quoted in David J. Garrow, *Bearing the Cross* (New York, 1984), p. 676. Kennedy quoted in Arthur Schlesinger, Jr., *A Thousand Days* (Boston, 1965), p. 970.

2. Viorst, *Fire in the Streets*, p. 227. A. Philip Randolph quote and march statistics in *New York Times*, August 29, 1963, pp. 16–17, 21. King on changes in speech in Garrow, *Bearing the Cross*, p. 283.

3. Advance Text of Speech to be Delivered by Martin Luther King, Jr., at March on Washington, August 28, 1963. CBS television footage makes it possible to compare what King said with his advance text.

4. King, Advance Text.

5. *Ibid*. See also Robert N. Bellah, "Civil Religion in America," in William G. McLoughlin and Robert N. Bellah, eds., *Religion in America* (Boston, 1968), pp. 3–11.

6. CBS coverage of "I Have a Dream." Isaiah, Verse 40, "News of the Returning Exiles."

7. CBS coverage of "I Have a Dream."

8. James Reston, "I Have a Dream," *New York Times*, August 29, 1963, p. 1.

9. Garrow, *Bearing the Cross*, 266–276.

10. *Ibid.*, p. 284.

11. For a profile of the march sponsors, see *New York Times*, August 29, 1963, p. 21.

12. Garrow, *Bearing the Cross*, pp. 146–149, 243–245, 267. King quoted in *New York Times*, June 10, 1963, pp. 1, 20.

13. Garrow, *Bearing the Cross*, pp. 271, 278. Kennedy meeting with march sponsors in Schlesinger, *A Thousand Days*, pp. 969, 970, 972. Kennedy news conference reported in *New York Times*, July 18, 1963, pp. 1, 10.

14. Henry Hampton and Steve Fayer, eds., *Voices of Freedom: An Oral History of the Civil Rights Movement form the 1950s through the 1980s* (New York, 1990), pp. 161, 169. Kennedy quoted in *New York Times*, August 29, 1963, p. 16.

15. Social Science survey in Viorst, *Fire in the Streets*, p. 230. *New York Times*, August 28, 1963, pp. 1, 21. *New York Times*, August 26, 1963, p. 21. *Newsweek*, September 9, 1963, pp. 19–22. *The Autobiography of Malcolm X* (New York, 1965), pp. 281, 280.

16. *New York Times Magazine*, August 25, 1963, pp. 1, 8–9, 57, 60–61. Garrow, *Bearing the Cross*, p. 278.

17. Notes taken at meeting of Mississippi Community Foundation in McComb, June 27, 1991. Claude Sitton, "Eight Negroes Freed in Registry Drive," *New York Times*, April 5, 1963, p. 16. Taylor Branch, *Parting the Waters: America in the King Years, 1954–63* (New York, 1988), pp. 512–513, 717–720.

18. Text of the speech Lewis gave at the March on Washington in *The Student Voice*, October 1963, p. 1.

19. *Ibid.*, pp. 1, 4.

20. Interview with Courtland Cox, March 28, 1991. Garrow, *Bearing the Cross*, pp. 281–283. James Forman, *The Making of Black Revolutionaries* (New York, 1972), pp. 334–335. Tom Kahn's help with the speech, Lewis notes, came primarily through informal talks in the week before the march. Interview with John Lewis, June 1988. SNCC Papers: John Lewis, "Six Month Report to SNCC Coordinating Committee," December 27, 1963, A-I-40, Reel 2.

21. Interview with John Lewis, June 1988. Carson, *In Struggle*, pp. 92–93. Viorst, *Fire in the Streets*, p. 109.

22. The original text for Lewis's "Speech at the March on Washington," SNCC Papers, A-I-42, Reel 2. Forman, *The Making of Black Revolutionaries*, p. 336.

23. Tom Wolfe, *Radical Chic and Mau-Mauing the Flak Catchers* (New York, 1970), pp. 97, 98, 120. Lewis, original text for "Speech at the March on Washington."

24. Lewis, original text for "Speech at the March on Washington."

25. SNCC Papers: Eleanor Holmes, "Confidential Memorandum," September 6, 1963, A-II-2, Reel 3. Holmes later married and became Eleanor Holmes Norton. Lewis, "Six Month Report to SNCC Coordinating Committee."

3. Tremor in the Iceberg

1. Bob Moses, Letter from the Magnolia Jail, November 1, 1961, in Tom Hayden, *Revolution in Mississippi*, SDS Publication, January 1962, p. 4.

2. Elizabeth Sutherland, ed., *Letters from Mississippi* (New York, 1965), p. 135. The volunteer's biblical reference is to Amos as a biblical rebel against authority.

3. Bob Moses quoted in Atwater, "If We Can Crack Mississippi," p. 16.

4. Interview with Hollis Watkins, August 8, 1991.

5. John Lewis quoted in Atwater, "If We Can Crack Mississippi," p. 19. *Jackson Daily News* quoted in Loewen and Sallis, *Mississippi: Conflict and Change*, p. 147. *Columbus Democrat* quoted in Vernon Lane Wharton, *The Negro in Mississippi, 1865–1890* (New York, 1965), p. 182. *Jackson Clarion-Ledger*, August 14, 1890, quoted in Randall Kennedy, "Keep the Nigger Down: The Age of Segregation in Mississippi," *Reconstruction*, 1, No. 3, 1991, 118.

6. Neil R. McMillen, *Dark Journey: Black Mississippians in the Age of Jim Crow* (Urbana, Ill., 1989), pp. 142–149. James K. Vardaman quoted in James W. Silver, *Mississippi: The Closed Society* (New York, 1966), p. 19. Eugene Bilbo quoted in Loewen and Sallis, *Mississippi: Conflict and Change*, p. 239.

7. Ross Barnett quoted in Silver, *Mississippi: The Closed Society*, p. 25. Loewen and Sallis, *Mississippi: Conflict and Change*, pp. 265, 149. McMillen, "Black Enfranchisement," p. 352. Paul Johnson, Jr., quoted in Cagin and Dray, *We Are Not Afraid*, p. 211.

8. Loewen and Sallis, *Mississippi: Conflict and Change*, pp. 178, 257–258. Walker Percy, "Mississippi: The Fallen Paradise," *Harper's* (April 1965), p. 166. Judge Bromfield quoted in Hayden, *Revolution in Mississippi*, p. 3. Brauer, *John F. Kennedy and the Second Reconstruction*, p. 264.

9. McAdam, *Freedom Summer*, p. 25. William McCord, *Mississippi: The Long Hot Summer* (New York, 1965), p. 42. Sutherland, *Letters from Mississippi*, p. 53. Fannie Lou Hamer, *To Praise Our Bridges* (Jackson, Miss., 1967), p. 11. Mamie E. Locke, "Is This America? Fannie Lou Hamer and the Mississippi Freedom Democratic Party," in Darlene Clark Hine, ed., *Black Women in United States History*, Vol. 16. Vicki L. Crawford, Jacqueline Anne Rouse, and Barbara Woods, eds., *Women in the Civil Rights*

Movement: Trailblazers and Torchbearers, 1941–1965 (Brooklyn, 1990), pp. 27–37. Bob Moses, "Letter to Northern Supporters," in Joanne Grant, ed., *Black Protest* (New York, 1968), p. 300.

10. Howard Zinn Papers, Notes on Mississippi Staff Meeting, November 1963, p. 11. Juan Williams, *Eyes on the Prize: America's Civil Rights Years, 1954–1965* (New York, 1987), p. 208. Anne Moody, *Coming of Age in Mississippi* (New York, 1968), p. 32. McCord, *Mississippi: The Long Hot Summer*, p. 42. McAdam, *Freedom Summer*, pp. 25–26.

11. Bob Moses quoted in *New America* (February 6, 1963), p. 5.

12. On June 27 and 28, 1991, veterans of the McComb civil rights movement gathered in McComb to retell their story. My account of events there reflects my notes of that meeting. Branch, *Parting the Waters*, p. 493.

13. Cagin and Dray, *We Are Not Afraid*, pp. 145–155.

14. Branch, *Parting the Waters*, p. 514.

15. Carson, *In Struggle*, pp. 49–50.

16. Bob Moses, "Mississippi: 1961–62," *Liberation*, January 1970, p. 14. Branch, *Parting the Waters*, pp. 520–521.

17. Moses, "Mississippi," p. 15. U.S. Congress, House Committee on the Judiciary, *Civil Rights Hearings*, 88th Congress, 1st Session (May 28, 1963), p. 1278. Moses quoted in Watters and Cleghorn, *Climbing Jacob's Ladder*, p. 65.

18. Forman, *The Making of Black Revolutionaries*, pp. 283–287. Cagin and Dray, *We Are Not Afraid*, p. 188.

19. Carson, *In Struggle*, p. 80. Branch, *Parting the Waters*, p. 713. Cagin and Dray, *We Are Not Afraid*, p. 190. Bob Moses, "Letter to Northern Supporters," February 27, 1963, in Grant, *Black Protest*, p. 300.

20. Cagin and Dray, *We Are Not Afraid*, pp. 191–192.

21. Claude Sitton, "Police Break Up Negroes' Rally," *New York Times*, March 28, 1963, p. 4. Claude Sitton, "Police Loose a Dog on Negroes Group," *New York Times*, March 29, 1963, pp. 1, 4. Claude Sitton, "Eight Negroes Freed in Registry Drive," *New York Times*, April 5, 1963, p. 16. Branch, *Parting the Waters*, pp. 721–725.

22. Carson, *In Struggle*, p. 97. David Harris, *Dreams Die Hard* (New York, 1982), pp. 33–34, 40–42.

23. Carson, *In Struggle*, pp. 96–97. Anne Romaine Interview with Bob Moses, Part II, pp. 13–14.

24. Bob Moses letter to Allard Lowenstein quoted in Harris, *Dreams Die Hard*, p. 40. Carson, *In Struggle*, pp. 96–98. Forman, *The Making of Black Revolutionaries*, pp. 354–356.

25. Harris, *Dreams Die Hard*, p. 42. Lawrence Guyot and Mike Thelwell, "The Politics of Necessity and Survival in Mississippi," *Freedomways* (Spring 1966), pp. 131–132.

26. Ivanhoe Donaldson quoted in Forman, *The Making of Black Revolutionaries*, p. 356.

27. Anne Romaine Interview with Bob Moses, Part I, p. 4.

28. *Ibid.*, Part II, p. 18. Letter from Wiley Branton quoted in Watters and Cleghorn, *Climbing Jacob's Ladder*, p. 213.

29. Howard Zinn Papers, Notes on Mississippi Staff Meeting, November 1963, pp. 5, 7. King, *Freedom Song*, p. 226.

30. Howard Zinn Papers, Notes on Mississippi Staff Meeting, November 1963, pp. 6, 19, 37.

31. *Ibid.*, pp. 21, 25, 9.

32. *Ibid.*, pp. 28, 37A, 37.

33. *Ibid.*, pp. 29, 33.

34. *Ibid.*, pp. 39, 41, 40.

35. Charlie Cobb quoted in Howell Raines, *My Soul Is Rested* (New York, 1977), p. 287.

36. *Ibid.*, p. 286.

37. Bob Moses at SNCC's April 1963 meeting in Atlanta quoted in Forman, *The Making of Black Revolutionaries*, p. 306. Howard Zinn Papers, Notes on Mississippi Staff Meeting, November 1963, pp. 16, 11.

38. Anne Romaine Interview with Bob Moses, Part II, pp. 18, 19.

39. Howard Zinn Papers, Notes on Mississippi Staff Meeting, November 1963, p. 22.

40. *Ibid.*, pp. 21, 24, 27, 31. Moses also quoted in Robert Penn Warren, *Who Speaks for the Negro?* (New York, 1966), p. 96. The February 12, 1964, date for that interview is given in Robert Penn Warren, "Two for SNCC," *Commentary*, April 1965, p. 38.

41. Howard Zinn Papers, Notes on Mississippi Staff Meeting, November 1963, pp. 31, 44, 27, 28.

42. Interview with Lawrence Guyot, March 26, 1991. SHSW: Howard Zinn Papers, Notes on Mississippi Staff Meeting, November 1963, pp. 6–7, 33, 36. Jerry DeMuth, "Tired of Being Sick and Tired," *Nation*, June 1, 1964, pp. 548–551.

43. Curtis Hayes now uses the name Curtis Muhammad. Willie Peacock now uses the name Wazir Peacock. In describing them in 1964 I have used the names they were known by then. Howard Zinn, *SNCC: The New Abolitionists* (Boston, 1964), pp. 187–189.

44. Interview with MacArthur Cotton, June 29, 1991. Interview with Curtis Hayes Muhammad, July 17, 1991.

4. Nobody's Cannon Fodder

1. Howard Zinn Papers, Notes on Mississippi Staff Meeting, November 1963, pp. 3, 5.

2. Sutherland, *Letters from Mississippi*, p. 17.

3. John Kennedy Inaugural Address, January 20, 1961. Sutherland, *Letters from Mississippi*, p. 16. Paul Cowan, *The Making of an Un-American*

(New York, 1970), p. 28. MLK: Summer Project Application Form. Margaret Aley now uses her married name Margaret Aley Chavez. Interview with Margaret Aley Chavez, August 24, 1991.

4. Text of John Kennedy Civil Rights Speech, June 11, 1963, in *New York Times*, June 12, 1963, p. 20. Branch, *Parting the Waters*, p. 821.

5. Interview with Pat Vail, February 23, 1992. Sutherland, *Letters from Mississippi*, p. 19.

6. SNCC Papers: Dear Summer Project Worker Letter, May 5, 1964, A-XV-180, Reel 39. On Kennedy and *The Other America* see Schlesinger, *A Thousand Days*, p. 1010. Michael Harrington, *Fragments of the Century* (New York, 1973), pp. 64–66. Michael Harrington, *The Other America* (Baltimore, 1969), p. 24.

7. Harrington, *The Other America*, pp. 170, 23, 164–168, 24.

8. *Ibid.*, p. 170. MLK: Summer Project Application. Sally Belfrage, *Freedom Summer* (New York, 1965), p. 7.

9. Martin Luther King, Jr., "Letter from Birmingham Jail," in *Why We Can't Wait* (New York, 1964), p. 77.

10. MLK: Summer Project Application. Sutherland, *Letters from Mississippi*, p. 17. Martin Luther King, Jr., *Stride Toward Freedom* (New York, 1958), p. 194.

11. Sutherland, *Letters from Mississippi*, pp. 19, 29.

12. Pam Parker now uses the name Chude Pam Allen. Interview with Chude Pam Allen, September 7, 1991. Barney Frank quoted in Atwater, "If We Can Crack Mississippi," p. 16. McAdam, *Freedom Summer*, pp. 40–42. Sutherland, *Letters from Mississippi*, p. 16.

13. SHSW: Sandra Hard Papers, Statement of Frank Cieciorka, September 8, 1964.

14. Interview with Robbie Osman, August 23, 1991. Sutherland, *Letters from Mississippi*, p. 23.

15. Interview with Frank Roosevelt, February 13, 1992. Sutherland, *Letters from Mississippi*, p. 23. Southern volunteer quoted in Belfrage, *Freedom Summer*, p. 7.

16. Sutherland, *Letters from Mississippi*, pp. 135, 22–23.

17. Cowan, *The Making of an Un-American*, p. 29. Interview with Dennis Flannigan, July 10, 1991.

18. Sam Walker quoted in Atwater, "If We Can Crack Mississippi," p. 17. Interview with Marshall Ganz, July 31, 1991. Summer Project Application Form.

19. Robert Coles, "We Shall Overcome," *New Republic*, July 11, 1964, pp. 13, 14. McAdam, *Freedom Summer*, p. 43.

5. Open the Eyes of the Nation

1. James Forman quoted in *Life*, July 3, 1964, p. 32b. J. Edgar Hoover from *Eyes on the Prize*, Part 5, "Is This America?"

2. SHSW: Eugene Nelson Papers, Eugene Nelson, Letter, July 26, 1964.

3. Louis Harris Survey in *Newsweek*, July 13, 1964, p. 24.

4. Howard Zinn Papers, SNCC Staff Meeting Minutes, June 9–11, 1964, p. 30.

5. Interview with Charlie Cobb, July 18, 1991. Interview with Sam Block, July 20, 1991. Interview with Curtis Hayes Muhammad, July 17, 1991.

6. Bob Robertson, "Militant Plan to Create Crisis in Mississippi," *San Francisco Chronicle*, December 7, 1963, p. 4.

7. SNCC Papers: Minutes of the Meeting of the SNCC Executive Committee, December 27–31, 1963, A-II-4, Reel 3, pp. 29, 28.

8. SNCC Papers: Meeting, Evening of January 24, 1964, A-III-1, Reel 38, pp. 1–3.

9. Bob Moses quoted from a talk given at the farm of E. W. Steptoe, Jr., in Amite County, Mississippi, June 29, 1991. See also Branch, *Parting the Waters*, pp. 520–521. Bob Moses, Letter to John Doar, Civil Rights Division, Justice Department, August 2, 1962.

10. Howard Zinn Papers, SNCC Staff Meeting Minutes, June 9–11, 1964, pp. 2, 29–32.

11. Ivanhoe Donaldson quoted in *New Yorker*, April 11, 1964, p. 35.

12. Bob Moses quoted in Robert Penn Warren, "Two for SNCC," p. 41. Hollis Watkins quoted in SHSW: Howard Zinn Papers, SNCC Staff Meeting Minutes, June 9-11, 1964, p. 30.

13. Bob Moses quoted in Belfrage, *Freedom Summer*, pp. 10, 26. Joseph Alsop, *Washington Post*, June 29, 1964, p. A17.

14. Howard Zinn Papers, SNCC Staff Meeting Minutes, June 9–11, 1964, pp. 15, 31.

15. King, *Freedom Song*, p. 369.

16. SNCC Papers: Memo to Accepted Volunteers, A-XV-189, Reel 39. Mississippi Summer Project Committee, Guidelines for Interviewing, April 14, 1964, A-XV-55, Reel 38.

17. Atwater, "If We Can Crack Mississippi," p. 16. SNCC Papers: Dorothy Zellner, Dear Friends of SNCC and Freedom Center People Letter, May 7, 1964, A-XV-188, Reel 39. King, *Freedom Song*, p. 369.

18. Interview with Wazir Peacock, July 9, 1991. SNCC Staff Meeting Minutes, June 9–11, 1964, p. 31.

19. Tracy Sugarman, *Stranger at the Gates* (New York, 1966), pp. 1–22. Belfrage, *Freedom Summer*, pp. 3–27. SHSW: Lisa Vogel Papers, Notes at 1964 Orientation, June 22–26, 1964.

20. Sugarman, *Stranger at the Gates*, p. 1. Belfrage, *Freedom Summer*,

p. 3. Alice Lake, "Last Summer in Mississippi," *Redbook*, November 1964, p. 112.

21. SHSW: Elizabeth Sutherland Papers, Karol Nelson, "Letter to Mom, Dad, and Vickie," June 22, 1964. Geoff Cowan, "Getting Ready," *Esquire*, September 1964, p. 105. Margaret Aley Chavez Letters (copies in author's possession), Margaret Aley, Letter, June 23, 1964. Belfrage, *Freedom Summer*, p. 23.

22. Sutherland, *Letters from Mississippi*, p. 22. SHSW: Elizabeth Sutherland Papers, Peggie Dobbie, "Letter to Mom and Dad," June 23, 1964.

23. Interview with Dennis Flannigan, July 10, 1991. Kathie Amatniek quoted in Sara Evans, *Personal Politics: The Roots of Women's Liberation in the Civil Rights Movement and the New Left* (New York, 1980), p. 70. Interview with Lisa Anderson, now Lisa Anderson Todd, February 10, 1992.

24. Sutherland, *Letters from Mississippi*, pp. 4, 2. SHSW: William Hodes Papers, William Hodes, Letter, June 16, 1964.

25. Sutherland, *Letters from Mississippi*, pp. 3–4. Interview with Heather Tobis, now Heather Tobis Booth, August 18, 1991.

26. Sutherland, *Letters from Mississippi*, p. 3. Rosellen Brown, *Civil Wars* (New York, 1984), p. 40.

27. Belfrage, *Freedom Summer*, pp. 15, 81, 80.

28. SHSW: William Hodes Papers, William Hodes, Letter, June 16, 1964. Sugarman, *Stranger at the Gates*, pp. 16–18.

29. William Hodes Papers, William Hodes, Letter, June 16, 1964.

30. *Ibid.*

31. Sutherland, *Letters from Mississippi*, p. 7. SHSW: Patrick Thomas Papers, Patrick Thomas, Letter, June 25, 1964.

32. Belfrage, *Freedom Summer*, p. 14. Sutherland, *Letters from Mississippi*, p. 28.

33. SHSW: Staughton Lynd Papers, Kirsty Powell, "A Report, Mainly on Ruleville Freedom School," Summer Project, 1964.

6. There May Be More Deaths

1. King, *Freedom Song*, pp. 377–379.

2. Cagin and Dray, *We Are Not Afraid*, pp. 34–35, 1–7.

3. King, *Freedom Song*, p. 379.

4. FBI Report on Andrew Goodman, NY 44-109, 7/2/64, MIBURN. Cagin and Dray, *We Are Not Afraid*, pp. 41–44.

5. Don Whitehead, *Attack on Terror: The FBI Against the Ku Klux Klan in Mississippi* (New York, 1970), p. 63.

6. Bob Moses quoted in Belfrage, *Freedom Summer*, pp. 25–26.

7. Claude Sitton, "Wreckage Raises New Fears over Fate of the Missing Men," *New York Times*, June 24, 1964, pp. 1, 20. William Bradford Huie,

Three Lives for Mississippi (New York, 1965), p. 145. Cagin and Dray, *We Are Not Afraid*, pp. 231, 235.

8. *Life*, July 3, 1964, pp. 32–34b. Interview with Mary King, July 12, 1991. Rainey quoted in Claude Sitton, "3 in Rights Drive Reported Missing," *New York Times*, June 23, 1964, p. 13. Paul Johnson, Jr., quoted in *Jackson Clarion-Ledger*, June 27, 1964, p. 1. *Birmingham News* story in Huie, *Three Lives for Mississippi*, p. 196.

9. CBS News, Transcript of "The Search in Mississippi," June 25, 1964, pp. 13–14, 23, 24, 12, 30.

10. *Ibid.*, p. 23.

11. "Sends Ex-CIA Head to South After Seeing Parents of Youths," *New York Times*, June 24, 1963, pp. 1, 21. Cagin and Dray, *We Are Not Afraid*, pp. 331–335. Interview with John Doar, February 25, 1992. Interview with Bill Moyers, May 11, 1992.

12. SNCC Papers: Council of Federated Organizations, *Mississippi Newsletter*, November 25, 1963, A-XV-114, Reel 39. Theodore H. White, *The Making of the President 1964* (New York, 1964), pp. 174–177. Cagin and Dray, *We Are Not Afraid*, p. 318. Lyndon Johnson quoted in Michael Oreskes, "Civil Rights Act Leaves Deep Mark on the American Political Landscape," *New York Times*, July 2, 1989, p. 16.

13. Lyndon Johnson, Address on Civil Rights Bill, *New York Times*, July 3, 1964, p. 9.

14. John Lewis quoted in *The Student Voice*, June 30, 1964, p. 2. Rita Schwerner quoted in Len Holt, *The Summer That Didn't End* (New York, 1965), p. 30.

15. Cowan, *The Making of an Un-American*, p. 28. SHSW: Stephen Bingham Papers, Stephen Bingham, "Mississippi Letter," February 15, 1965. Belfrage, *Freedom Summer*, p. 12.

16. Sutherland, *Letters from Mississippi*, pp. 33, 26–27. Interview with Nancy Jervis, June 17, 1991. Margaret Aley Chavez Letters, Margaret Aley, Letter, June 23, 1964.

17. SHSW: Ellen Lake Papers, Ellen Lake, Letter, June 20, 1964.

18. Sandra Hard Papers, Sandra Hard, "Statement of Sandra Hard," September 8, 1964. Chude Pam Allen Letters (copies in author's possession), Pam Parker, Letter, June 30, 1964.

19. Cleveland Sellers with Robert Terrell, *The River of No Return* (New York, 1973), p. 82. Bob Moses quoted in Belfrage, *Freedom Summer*, p. 26.

7. The Magnolia Jungle

1. David Halberstam, "Hostility Meets Rights Workers," *New York Times*, July 3, 1964, p. 8. SHSW: SDS Papers, Herschel Kaminsky, Letter, September 15, 1964. SNCC Papers: Bob Moses, "Memo to Friends of

Freedom in Mississippi," A-XV-180, Reel 39. Bob Moses, "To: Parents of All Mississippi Summer Volunteers," A-XV-167, Reel 39.

2. Moses, "To: Parents of All Mississippi Volunteers."

3. SNCC Papers: Mississippi Summer Project Committee, "Memo to Accepted Applicants, A-XV-189, Reel 39. SHSW: Ellen Lake Papers, Security Handbook.

4. *Jackson Clarion-Ledger*, June 30 and June 19, 1964. Newspaper quotes from Shirley Tucker, ed., *Mississippi from Within* (New York, 1965), pp. 10, 39. Paul Johnson, Jr., quoted in McCord, *Mississippi: The Long Hot Summer*, p. 47.

5. SNCC Papers: Student Nonviolent Coordinating Committee, "Mississippi Legislates to Outlaw Summer Civil Rights Project," A-XV-180, Reel 39. COFO, "The Mississippi Legislature," June 2, 1964, A-XV-176, Reel 39.

6. SHSW: John R. Salter Papers, Medgar Evers, Radio Speech on WLBT and WJTV, May 20, 1963. "Allen's Army," *Newsweek*, February 24, 1964, p. 30. John Dittmer, "The Politics of the Mississippi Movement, 1954–1964," in Charles W. Eagles, ed., *The Civil Rights Movement in America* (Jackson, Miss., 1987), pp. 65–93.

7. "Allen's Army," *Newsweek*, February 24, 1964, p. 30. Senator Stennis quoted in *Washington Post*, June 25, 1964, p. A3. Mayor Burt quoted in Atwater, "If We Can Crack Mississippi," p. 19.

8. *Klan Ledger* quoted in Sutherland, *Letters from Mississippi*, p. 119. National States' Rights party quoted in McCord, *Mississippi: The Long Hot Summer*, p. 48.

9. Whitehead, *Attack on Terror*, p. 100. "God Help the USA," *Meridian Star*, July 12, 1964, p. 4A.

10. Heidi Dole quoted in Belfrage, *Freedom Summer*, p. 28. Eugene Nelson quoted in Jerry Demuth, "Summer in Mississippi," *Nation*, September 14, 1964, p. 110.

11. Sutherland, *Letters from Mississippi*, pp. 8, 36, 37. Elizabeth Sutherland Papers, Jan Handke, Letter, June 25, 1964.

12. Margaret Aley Chavez Letters, Margaret Aley, Letter, June 28, 1964. Phil Moore quoted in Mary Aicken Rothschild, *A Case of Black and White: Northern Volunteers and the Southern Freedom Summers, 1964–65* (Westport, Conn., 1982), p. 59.

13. Elizabeth Sutherland Papers, Clark Gardener, Letter, n.d. Marshall Ganz Interview, July 31, 1991. Robbie Osman Interview, August 23, 1991.

14. Interview with Nancy Jervis, June 17, 1991. Elizabeth Sutherland Papers, Nancy Schieffelin, Letter, n.d.

15. Elizabeth Sutherland Papers, Jacques Calma, Letter, n.d. Interview with Lewis Hyde, June 4, 1991. Ron de Souza, "Mississippi Diary," copy in author's possession, p. 2. Phil Moore quoted in Rothschild, *A Case of Black and White*, p. 59.

16. Interview with Dennis Flannigan, July 10, 1991. Sutherland, *Letters*

from Mississippi, pp. 149, 151. Peter Cummings, "The Mississippi Summer Project," *Harvard Crimson*, Registration Issue, 1964. Interview with Linda Davis, February 19, 1992. Belfrage, *Freedom Summer*, p. 44.

17. SNCC Papers: Interview with Ron Ridenour, June 24, 1964, A-XV-170, Reel 39. Margaret Aley Chavez Letters, Margaret Aley, Letter, July 21, 1964. Margaret Aley, "Abuse in a Dixie Jail," *San Francisco Chronicle*, July 22, 1964.

18. Ellen Lake Papers, Ellen Lake, Letter, July 4, 1964.

19. Peggy Dobbie quoted in *Pembroke Record*, September 25, 1964. Belfrage, *Freedom Summer*, p. 31. Margaret Aley Chavez Letters, Margaret Aley, Letter, July 2, 1964.

20. Sutherland, *Letters from Mississippi*, pp. 56, 39, 55. Interview with Heather Tobis Booth, August 18, 1991.

21. Interview with Pat Vail, February 23, 1992. Sutherland, *Letters from Mississippi*, p. 42.

22. *Ibid.*, pp. 53, 54–55, 62.

23. SHSW: Christopher Wilson Papers, Christopher Wilson, Letter, July 3, 1964.

24. SHSW: Robert Feinglass Papers, Robert Feinglass, Letter, n.d. Charles Payne, "Men Led, but Women Organized: Movement Participation of Women in the Mississippi Delta," in Crawford, Rouse, and Woods, *Women in the Civil Rights Movement*, pp. 1–11.

25. Eugene Nelson Papers, Eugene Nelson, Letter, July 3, 1964. Ellen Lake, Letter, July 26, 1964.

26. Sutherland, *Letters from Mississippi*, p. 44. Belfrage, *Freedom Summer*, p. 75.

27. Paul and Geoff Cowan, "And Three Letters from Mississippi," *Esquire*, September 1964, p. 190.

28. Sutherland, *Letters from Mississippi*, pp. 48, 44.

29. Interview with Margaret Aley Chavez, August 24, 1991. Bob Moses quoted in Belfrage, *Freedom Summer*, p. 10.

8. Pinto Beans and Politics

1. Unita Blackwell quoted in Hampton and Fayer, *Voices of Freedom*, p. 193.

2. Bob Moses testimony in House Committee on the Judiciary, *Civil Rights Hearings*, p. 1278.

3. Interview with Charlie Cobb, July 18, 1991. SNCC Papers: Charlie Cobb, "Prospectus for a Summer Freedom School Program," December 1963, A-VIII-122, Reel 20. McAdam, *Freedom Summer*, pp. 25–26.

4. Cobb, "Prospectus for a Summer Freedom School Program."

5. *Ibid.* SNCC Papers: Charlie Cobb, Memo to SNCC Executive Committee, January 14, 1964. A-VIII-122, Reel 20. McAdam, *Freedom Summer*,

p. 83. Daniel Pearlstein, "Teaching Freedom: SNCC and the Creation of the Mississippi Freedom Schools," *History of Education Quarterly*, 30 (Fall 1990), 308–312.

6. Staughton Lynd, "The Freedom Schools: Concept and Organization," *Freedomways*, 5 (Spring 1966), 302–304. Howard Zinn, "Schools in Context: The Mississippi Idea," *Nation*, November 23, 1964, p. 371.

7. Sutherland, *Letters from Mississippi*, pp. 98, 110, 100, 114. Zinn, "Schools in Context," p. 371.

8. Elizabeth Sutherland Papers, Nancy Schieffelin, Letter, July 6, 1964. SNCC Papers: "Freedom School Report," A-IV-175, Reel 6. SHSW: Staughton Lynd Papers, Powell, "A Report, Mainly on Ruleville Freedom School," p. 4.

9. Sutherland, *Letters from Mississippi*, pp. 101, 96, 98.

10. Zinn, "Schools in Context," pp. 371–375. *The Student Voice*, August 5, 1964, p. 2.

11. SNCC Papers: Letter, July 11, 1964, Appendix A-370, Reel 68. Sutherland, *Letters from Mississippi*, p. 97. Chude Pam Allen Letters, Pam Parker, Letter, n.d.

12. Chude Pam Allen Letters, Pam Parker, Letter, n.d. Karol Nelson quoted in Lake, "Last Summer in Mississippi," p. 116.

13. SNCC Papers: *1964 Platform of the Mississippi Freedom School Convention*, Appendix A-334, Reel 67. Lynd, "The Freedom Schools," p. 304. SNCC Papers: Staughton Lynd, Letter, March 25, 1964, Appendix A-500, Reel 69. SNCC Papers: Liz Fusco, "Freedom Schools in Mississippi, 1964," A-XV-165, Reel 39. SNCC Papers: Alvin Pam, "Report on the Summer Project," July 8, 1964, A-IV-175, Reel 6.

14. Bob Moses quoted in Belfrage, *Freedom Summer*, p. 10. Profiles of Freedom Schools from the papers of Summer Project volunteer Margaret Dobbins (copy in author's possession). McAdam, *Freedom Summer*, p. 26.

15. U.S. Commission on Civil Rights, *Hearings on Civil Rights*, p. 161.

16. SHSW: Charles Stewart Papers, Charles Stewart, "Report on the Mississippi Summer Project—1964," September 1964, p. 5. U.S. Commission on Civil Rights, *Hearings on Civil Rights*, p. 157.

17. Sandra Hard Papers, Les Johnson, "Excerpts from Mississippi Letters." Robert Feinglass Papers, Robert Feinglass, Letter, n.d.

18. Sutherland, *Letters from Mississippi*, pp. 80–81.

19. SNCC Papers: Geoff Cowan, "Letter from the South," A-XV-175, Reel 39. Stewart, "Report on the Mississippi Summer Project—1964," p. 2.

20. Ellen Lake Papers, Ellen Lake, Letter, June 29, 1964.

21. William Hodes Papers, William Hodes, Letter, July 22, 1964. Stewart, "Report on the Mississippi Summer Project—1964," p. 4.

22. Johnson, "Excerpts from Mississippi Letters." Nancy Jervis Interview, June 17, 1991.

23. Sutherland, *Letters from Mississippi*, pp. 81, 87, 77.

24. Stuart Rawlings, *Mississippi Diary* (copy in author's possession), p. 68. Hodes, Letter, July 2, 1964. SHSW: Stephen Bingham Papers: Stephen Bingham, Mississippi Letter, February 15, 1965.

25. Sandra Hard Papers, Statement of Frank Cieciorka, September 8, 1964.

26. SHSW: Patrick Thomas Papers, Patrick Thomas, Letter, June 25, 1964.

27. Chalmers, "Committed, Proud, and Distrustful: The Mississippi Freedom Volunteers 20 Years Later," p. 38.

28. Bob Moses quoted in *New Yorker*, April 11, 1964, p. 36. SHSW: Anne Romaine Interview with Joseph Rauh, Jr., June 1967, pp. 1–2. Len Holt, *The Summer That Didn't End*, p. 154.

29. Carson, *In Struggle*, p. 109.

30. *Ibid.*, pp. 109–110.

31. *Ibid.*, pp. 108–109. Lawrence Guyot and Mike Thelwell, "Toward Independent Political Power," *Freedomways*, 6 (Summer 1966), 246–254. Holt, *The Summer That Didn't End*, pp. 158–162. Viorst, *Fire in the Streets*, p. 265. *The Student Voice*, August 12, 1964, pp. 1–2.

32. SNCC Papers: Bob Moses and FDP Coordinators, "Emergency Memorandum," July 19, 1964, A-XVI-30, Reel 41.

33. William Hodes Papers, William Hodes, Letter, July 22, 1964. Sutherland, *Letters from Mississippi*, p. 205.

34. McCord, *Mississippi: The Long Hot Summer*, p. 115. Carson, *In Struggle*, p. 98.

35. Belfrage, *Freedom Summer*, p. 186. Sutherland, *Letters from Mississippi*, pp. 210, 211. Christopher Wilson Papers, Christopher Wilson, Letter, July 31, 1964.,

36. Forman, *The Making of Black Revolutionaries*, p. 384. Holt, *The Summer That Didn't End*, p. 158. *The Student Voice*, August 12, 1964, pp. 1–4. McCord, *Mississippi: The Long Hot Summer*, p. 114.

9. No Two Seats

1. Forman, *The Making of Black Revolutionaries*, p. 384.

2. MFDP delegate Dewey Greene quoted in Belfrage, *Freedom Summer*, p. 228. Holt, *The Summer That Didn't End*, p. 170.

3. McCord, *Mississippi: The Long Hot Summer*, pp. 115–116.

4. Sutherland, *Letters from Mississippi*, p. 119. James Eastland quoted in Huie, *Three Lives for Mississippi*, pp. 217–218.

5. "Recovery of the Victims' Bodies at Olen Burrage's Dam on August 4, 1964," File 44-25706, Federal Bureau of Investigation, MIBURN. Whitehead, *Attack on Terror*, pp. 130–137.

6. Claude Sitton, "Graves at a Dam," *New York Times*, August 5, 1964, pp. 1, 37. Claude Sitton, "Experts Identify Mississippi Bodies as Rights

Aides," *New York Times*, August 6, 1964, pp. 1, 16. Claude Sitton, "Chaney Was Given a Brutal Beating," *New York Times*, August 8, 1964, p. 7. Dr. David Spain, "Mississippi Autopsy" in *Mississippi Eyewitness* (*Ramparts* Magazine, 1964), p. 49. SNCC Papers: Mississippi Summer Project, "Running Summary of Incidents," August 8, 1964, A-XV-180, Reel 39. Cagin and Dray, *We are not Afraid*, p. 408.

7. *Greenville Delta Democrat-Times* quoted in Whitehead, *Attack on Terror*, p. 141. Florence Mars, *Witness in Philadelphia* (Baton Rouge, 1977), p. 106. *Meridian Star* quoted in Claude Sitton, "Tragedy in Mississippi," *New York Times*, August 9, 1964, p. 6E. "The Mississippi Murders: 21 Arrests," *Newsweek*, December 14, 1964, p. 21.

8. Paul Johnson, Jr., quoted in Huie, *Three Lives for Mississippi*, pp. 225–226.

9. Mississippi Democratic Party Platform quoted in Rothschild, *A Case of Black and White*, p. 65.

10. David Dennis, Eulogy for James Chaney, in Williams, *Eyes on the Prize*, pp. 239–240. Holt, *The Summer That Didn't End*, p. 167. Ed Koch quoted in McAdam, *Freedom Summer*, p. 156.

11. "Mississippi's Delegates," *New York Times*, August 19, 1964, p. 36.

12. Interview with Pat Vail, February 23, 1992. Interview with Hollis Watkins, August 8, 1991. SHSW: SC 1069, Anne Romaine Interview with Joseph Rauh, Jr., June 1967, pp. 15–16.

13. LBJ: Meeting of the Credentials Committee, Democratic National Convention, August 22, 1964, pp. 42–43.

14. *Ibid.*, p. 63.

15. Viorst, *Fire in the Streets*, p. 263. Holt, *The Summer That Didn't End*, p. 169. SHSW: Anne Romaine Interview with Joseph Rauh, Jr., pp. 14, 18.

16. Edsall and Edsall, *Chain Reaction*, p. 36. Michael Oreskes, "Civil Rights Act Leaves Deep Mark on the American Political Landscape," *New York Times*, July 2, 1989, p. 16. Walter Reuther quoted by Joseph Rauh, Jr., in SHSW: Mss 579, *Freedom Summer Reviewed*, "Mississippi Freedom Democratic Party and the Atlantic City Convention," Tougaloo College, November 1, 1979, p. 28. Interview with Bill Moyers, May 11, 1992.

17. Interview with Frank Smith, March 27, 1991.

18. U.S. Senate, Select Committee to Study Governmental Operations with Respect to Intelligence Activities, *Final Report: Supplementary Detailed Staff Reports on Intelligence Activities and the Rights of Americans* (Washington, D.C., April 23, 1976), pp. 117–119. David Garrow, *The FBI and Martin Luther King* (New York, 1983), pp. 118–119. Curt Gentry, *J. Edgar Hoover: The Man and His Secrets* (New York, 1991), p. 578.

19. Belfrage, *Freedom Summer*, p. 237.

20. Weisbrot, *Freedom Bound*, p. 123. "Battle of Credentials," *Newsweek*, September 7, 1964, p. 26. E. W. Kenworthy, "Seating Panel Seeks a

Vow of Support," *New York Times*, August 24, 1964, pp. 1, 16. SHSW: Anne Romaine Interview with Joseph Rauh, Jr., pp. 11, 17–19. Rauh quoted in *Washington Post*, August 24, 1964, p. A10.

21. SHSW: Anne Romaine Interview with Joseph Rauh, Jr., pp. 7, 12, 17–18. For a discussion of Edith Green's proposal see SHSW: Mss 588, Howard Zinn Papers, Arthur Waskow, "Notes on the Democratic National Convention," August 1964, pp. 9–12. Interview with Fannie Lou Hamer, *Freedomways*, 5 (Spring 1965), 240.

22. Anne Romaine Interview with Joseph Rauh, Jr., pp. 17–18. Findlay Lewis, *Mondale: Portrait of an American Politician* (New York, 1980), p. 126.

23. Anne Romaine Interview with Joseph Rauh, Jr., p. 18. Lewis, *Mondale*, p. 126.

24. Anne Romaine Interview with Joseph Rauh, Jr., p. 19. Aaron Henry quoted in *Washington Post*, August 24, 1964, p. A10.

25. "Battle of Credentials," *Newsweek*, p. 26. Hubert Humphrey, *The Education of a Public Man* (Garden City, N.Y., 1976), p. 299.

26. Anne Romaine Interview with Joseph Rauh, Jr., pp. 19–20. Lewis, *Mondale*, p. 129. Rauh quoted in Cagin and Dray, *We Are Not Afraid*, p. 417.

27. Rauh quoted in *New York Times*, August 25, 1964, p. 23. Anne Romaine Interview with Joseph Rauh, Jr., p. 22. Holt, *The Summer That Didn't End*, p. 164.

28. Lewis, *Mondale*, pp. 130–131. Rauh quoted in *Freedom Summer Reviewed*, p. 34.

29. "Texts of Convention Committee Report and Mississippi Statement," *New York Times*, August 26, 1964, p. 28. "Credentials Committee Report on Mississippi," *Washington Post*, August 26, 1964, p. A2.

30. Lewis, *Mondale*, pp. 131–133.

31. Anne Romaine Interview with Joseph Rauh, Jr., pp. 25–26.

32. *Ibid.*, pp. 25–27. Laurence Stern, "Clash of Rauh's Convention Roles Hints Trouble with Administration," *Washington Post*, August 25, 1964, p. A7.

33. Anne Romaine Interview with Joseph Rauh, Jr., pp. 27–30. Lewis, *Mondale*, pp. 134–135.

34. SI: Civil Rights Documentation Project, Katherine Shannon Interview with Joseph Rauh, Jr., August 28, 1967, p. 74. SHSW: SC 1069, Anne Romaine Interview with Ed King, August 1966, pp. 7–9.

35. Anne Romaine Interview with Ed King, p. 9. Anne Romaine Interview with Joseph Rauh, Jr., pp. 30–32.

36. Anne Romaine Interview with Joseph Rauh, Jr., p. 33. Governor Paul Johnson, Jr., quoted in *New York Times*, August 26, 1964, p. 28. Waskow, "Notes on the Democratic National Convention," pp. 23–24.

37. Waskow, "Notes on the Democratic National Convention," p. 27. E. L. Kenworthy, "Mississippi Seats Taken by Negroes," *New York Times*, August 26, 1964, p. 28. Viorst, *Fire in the Streets*, p. 265.

38. Forman, *The Making of Black Revolutionaries*, pp. 390–395. Waskow, "Notes on the Democratic National Convention," pp. 29–31. Charles Sherrod, "Mississippi at Atlantic City," *Grain of Salt* (New York, Union Theological Seminary), October 12, 1964, pp. 4–11.

39. Forman, *The Making of Black Revolutionaries*, p. 392. Interview with Courtland Cox, May 28, 1991.

40. Forman, *The Making of Black Revolutionaries*, pp. 393–396.

41. *Ibid.*, pp. 395–396. Annie Devine quoted in Sherrod, "Mississippi at Atlantic City," *Grain of Salt*, pp. 6–7. MSRC: Robert Wright Interview with Unita Blackwell, August 10, 1968, p. 15.

42. MSRC: Robert Wright Interview with Fannie Lou Hamer, August 7, 1968, p. 29. Fannie Lou Hamer quoted in Forman, *The Making of Black Revolutionaries*, p. 395. Victoria Gray is now Victoria Gray Adams. Interview with Victoria Gray Adams, August 4, 1991. Garrow, *Bearing the Cross*, pp. 349–351.

43. Viorst, *Fire in the Streets*, pp. 266–267. Katherine Shannon Interview with Joseph Rauh, Jr., p. 77. Allard Lowenstein quoted in *The Stanford Daily*, May 28, 1965, p. 3.

44. Anthony Lewis, "The Negro and Politics," *New York Times*, August 27, 1964, p. 23.

45. Bayard Rustin quoted in Katherine Shannon Interview with Joseph Rauh, Jr., p. 74. Bayard Rustin, "From Protest to Politics: The Future of the Civil Rights Movement," *Commentary* (February 1965), pp. 31, 29.

46. Roy Wilkins, "Lost Victory in AC," *Amsterdam News*, September 5, 1964, p. 18.

47. Interview with Hollis Watkins, August 8, 1991. Julian Bond quoted in John Neary, *Julian Bond: Black Rebel* (New York, 1971), pp. 72–73. Forman, *The Making of Black Revolutionaries*, pp. 395–396.

48. Interview with Bob Moses, May 8, 1991. Stokely Carmichael quoted in Tom Brooks, *Walls Come Tumbling Down: A History of the Civil Rights Movement, 1940–1970* (Englewood Cliffs, N.J., 1974), p. 249. Stokely Carmichael, speaking as Kwame Touré at "We Shall Not Be Moved": Conference on the Life and Times of the Student Nonviolent Coordinating Committee, 1960–1966, Trinity College, Hartford, Conn., Session # 7, p. 46. Max Frankel, "Democrats to Seat Mississippi Rebels," *New York Times*, August 21, 1968, pp. 1, 32.

49. Lyndon Johnson, *The Vantage Point: Perspectives of the Presidency* (New York, 1971), p. 101. Sellers with Terrell, *The River of No Return*, p. 111.

10. Loose Ends

1. SNCC Papers: John Lewis Letter, August 19, 1964, A-XVII-61, Reel 42. Bob Moses quoted in W. F. Minor, "200 Volunteers to Stay in Mississippi

This Winter," *New Orleans Times-Picayune*, August 20, 1964, p. 30. John Herbers, "Civil Rights Drive Alters Mississippi," *New York Times*, August 20, 1964, pp. 1, 15. Richard Corrigan, "Summer Project Is Evaluated," *Washington Post*, August 23, 1964, p. A4. James Millstone, "Better Police Protection Called Most Important Gain in Summer of Rights Work in Mississippi," *St. Louis Post-Dispatch*, August 13, 1964, p. 2A.

2. Bob Moses quoted in Belfrage, *Freedom Summer*, p. 10.

3. Julian Bond quoted in Neary, *Julian Bond*, pp. 70–71.

4. SI: Voices of the Civil Rights Movement, Interview with Willie Peacock, February 1, 1980, p. 15. Bob Moses quoted in "Moses of Mississippi," *Pacific Scene*, 5 (February 1965), 4.

5. King, *Freedom Song*, pp. 437, 438.

6. Carson, *In Struggle*, pp. 134–136.

7. Hamer, *To Praise Our Bridges*, p. 21.

8. Forman, *The Making of Black Revolutionaries*, pp. 407, 411. Julian Bond quoted in Neary, *Julian Bond*, p. 73.

9. SNCC Papers: Rough Minutes of a Meeting Called by the National Council of Churches to Discuss the Mississippi Project, September 18, 1964, A-XVI-51, Reel 41.

10. Forman, *The Making of Black Revolutionaries*, pp. 414, 427.

11. SNCC Papers: Waveland Minutes, September 7, 1964, p. 3, A-V-18, Reel 11. For earlier SNCC fears about expansion, see Executive Committee of SNCC, Memorandum to All SNCC Project Heads, February 24, 1964.

12. Howard Zinn Papers, Notes on Mississippi Staff Meeting, November 1963, p. 36. SHSW: Stuart Ewen Papers, Silas Norman, Jr., "What Is the Importance of Racial Considerations Among the Staff?"

13. Norman, "What Is the Importance of Racial Considerations Among the Staff?"

14. SHSW: Charles Sherrod Papers, Maria Varela, "Training SNCC Staff to be Organizers."

15. Stuart Ewen Papers, Charles Sherrod, "Untitled Paper."

16. *Ibid.*

17. Moses's paper was unsigned, but he acknowledged which one it was. Interview with Bob Moses, May 7, 1991. Stuart Ewen Papers, Unsigned Paper.

18. John Herbers, "FBI Arrests 21 in Mississippi," *New York Times*, December 5, 1964, pp. 1, 18. Carson, *In Struggle*, p. 151.

19. SNCC Papers: John Lewis, "Statement at SNCC Staff Meeting," February 1965, A-I-40, Reel 2, pp. 1–2, 4.

20. *Ibid.*, pp. 3, 5, 4.

21. *Ibid.*, pp. 5–6, 7.

22. Bob Moses quoted in Notes on Mississippi Staff Meeting, November 1963, p. 40. SNCC quote from Gene Roberts, "Black Power Idea Long in Planning," *New York Times*, August 5, 1966, p. 10. Stokely

Carmichael and Charles V. Hamilton, *Black Power: The Politics of Liberation in America* (New York, 1967), p. 46. Lewis would soon represent a "go-slow conservatism" in the eyes of many younger SNCC field secretaries. Interview with Sam Howze, now known as Sala Udin, March 15, 1992.

23. Chude Pam Allen Letters, Pam Parker, Letter, August 27, 1964. The careful debriefing Moses had in mind would have involved almost as much preparation as the orientation in Ohio. Interview with Bob Moses, May 7, 1991.

24. SHSW: Sam Walker Papers, R. Hunter Morey, "Cross Roads in COFO," December 3, 1964. Forman, *The Making of Black Revolutionaries*, p. 420.

25. Interview with Chude Pam Allen, September 7, 1991. See also Robert Coles, "Social Struggle and Weariness," *Psychiatry*, 27 (November 1964), 305–315. (Copy of anonymous volunteer letter in author's possession.)

26. Sutherland, *Letters from Mississippi*, p. 195. Interview with Chude Pam Allen, September 7, 1991. Belfrage, *Freedom Summer*, p. 196.

27. Sutherland, *Letters from Mississippi*, p. 224. Interview with Nancy Jervis, June 17, 1991. Cummings, "The Mississippi Summer Project," pp. S-9, S-10. Interview with Lester Galt, August 15, 1991.

28. Interview with Chude Pam Allen, September 7, 1991. Interview with Nancy Schieffelin, June 3, 1991. Interview with Len Edwards, September 5, 1991. See also the Len Edwards interview in McAdam, *Freedom Summer*, p. 134.

29. Sutherland, *Letters from Mississippi*, p. 227. Eugene Nelson Papers, Eugene Nelson, Letter, August 2, 1964.

30. Anonymous volunteer letter, November 11, 1964, copy in author's possession. Interview with Nancy Schieffelin, June 3, 1964.

31. Interview with Nancy Schieffelin, July 12, 1991. Ellen Lake Papers, Ellen Lake, Letter, August 12, 1964.

32. Interview with Heather Tobis Booth, August 18, 1991. Interview with Chude Pam Allen, September 7, 1991.

33. Sutherland, *Letters from Mississippi*, p. 232. Interview with Lester Galt, August 15, 1991.

34. Interview with Linda Davis, February 19, 1992. Sutherland, *Letters from Mississippi*, p. 230. Marshall Ganz, petition to Administrative Board of Harvard College, August 31, 1964.

35. Interview with Margaret Aley Chavez, August 24, 1991. Ellen Lake Papers, Ellen Lake, Letter, August 12, 1964. Interview with Dennis Flannigan, July 10, 1991.

36. Vincent Harding quoted in Lake, "Last Summer in Mississippi," p. 117.

37. Cowan, *The Making of an Un-American*, p. 62.

38. MLK: Martin Luther King, Jr., Nobel Prize Acceptance Speech, December 10, 1964.

II. Mississippi Revisited

1. Cagin and Dray, *We Are Not Afraid*, pp. 408–409.

2. Dave Dennis quoted in Williams, *Eyes on the Prize*, pp. 239–240.

3. Kornbluth, "The '64 Civil Rights Murders," p. 60. Dudley Clendenin, "3 Rights Deaths' Legacy: Peace but No Consensus," *New York Times*, June 24, 1984, p. 16.

4. Interview with Dick Molpus, June 26, 1991. Dick Molpus quoted in Kornbluth, "The '64 Civil Rights Murders," pp. 54, 60.

5. Text of Dick Molpus Remarks, June 21, 1989.

6. Text of Ray Mabus Remarks, June 21, 1989. Kornbluth, "The '64 Civil Rights Murders," p. 18. Peter Boyer, "The Yuppies of Mississippi," *New York Times Magazine*, February 28, 1988, p. 24.

7. Interview with Dick Molpus, June 26, 1991.

8. Interview with Ray Mabus, June 27, 1991.

9. In the 1991 election Ray Mabus was defeated by Kirk Fordice, a conservative Republican who attacked quotas, welfare, and the Voting Rights Act. See Thomas Edsall, "Conservative Populist Challenges Mabus," *Washington Post*, November 5, 1991, p. A6. Frank R. Parker, *Black Votes Count: Political Empowerment in Mississippi After 1965* (Chapel Hill, 1990), p. 2. Mike Espy quoted in Boyer, "The Yuppies of Mississippi," p. 43. Peter Kilborn, "Charges of Exploitation Roil a Catfish Plant," *New York Times*, December 10, 1990, p. B10. Mississippi unemployment figures from Mississippi Employment Security Commission supplied during interview with Patsy Brumfield, January 10, 1992.

10. C. Vann Woodward, "What Happened to the Civil Rights Movement?" *Harper's*, January 1967, p. 34. Ronald Brownstein, "Beyond Quotas," *Los Angeles Times Magazine*, July 28, 1991, p. 38.

11. Woodward, "What Happened to the Civil Rights Movement?" p. 34. Executive Order 11375 cited in Paul Seabury, "HEW and the Universities," *Commentary*, February 1972, p. 39.

12. Nicholas Lemann, "How the Political War on the 'War on Poverty' Keeps America from Winning a Real Victory," *Washington Post*, May 10, 1992, pp. C1–C2. Nathan Glazer, "The Limits of Social Policy," *Commentary*, September 1971, pp. 51–58. Jefferson Morley, "Bush and the Blacks: An Unknown Story," *New York Review of Books*, January 16, 1992, p. 21.

13. Ronald Radosh, "From Civil Rights to Black Power: The Breakup of the Civil Rights Coalition," in Peter Collier and David Horowitz, eds., *Second Thoughts About Race in America* (Lanham, Md., 1992), pp. 13–14.

14. Orlando Patterson and Chris Winship, "White Poor, Black Poor," *New York Times*, May 3, 1992, p. E17. Jeffrey Schmalz, "Disaffection with National Leaders Sharpens in the Glare of Los Angeles," *New York Times*, May 10, 1992, p. E1. Sidney Blumenthal, "Firebell," *New Republic*, May 25, 1992, pp. 11–14. Forman, *The Making of Black Revolutionaries*, pp. 395–396.

15. John Lewis, "Statement at SNCC Staff Meeting," February 1965.

16. Bob Moses quoted in Warren, "Two for SNCC," p. 41. Julius Lester, *Look Out Whitey! Black Power's Gon' Get Your Mama!* (New York, 1969), p. 138. Carson, *In Struggle*, p. 37. Chicago Office of SNCC, "We Want Black Power," in August Meier, Elliott Rudwick, and Francis Broderick, eds., *Black Protest Thought in the Twentieth Century* (New York, 1971), p. 487.

17. John Lewis quoted in Joe Klein, "Race: The Issue," *New York*, May 29, 1989, pp. 34–35. Andrew Hacker, *Two Nations: Black and White, Separate, Hostile, Unequal* (New York, 1992), pp. 62–64.

18. Interview with Bob Moses, May 8, 1991. "Text of Convention Committee Report and Mississippi Statement," *New York Times*, August 26, 1964, p. 28. Max Frankel, "Democrats to Seat Mississippi Rebels," *New York Times*, August 21, 1968, pp. 1, 32. Richard L. Lyons, "Miss. Regulars Banned in Chicago," *Washington Post*, August 21, 1968, pp. A1, A8.

19. Adam Nossiter, "Whites Returning to Miss. Schools," *Atlanta Constitution*, October 5, 1990, pp. 1, 10. William Julius Wilson, "Race-Neutral Programs and the Democratic Coalition," *American Prospect*, Spring 1990, pp. 74–80.

Index

A Note on the Author

Nicolaus Mills was born in Cleveland, Ohio, and studied at Harvard and Brown universities. He has been a Woodrow Wilson Fellow and the recipient of a Rockefeller Humanities Fellowship, and is now Professor of American Studies at Sarah Lawrence College. He is also a co-editor of *Dissent* magazine. Mr. Mills's other books include *The New Journalism, The Great School Bus Controversy, The Crowd in American Literature,* and *Culture in an Age of Money.* He lives in New York City.